CORRUPTION OF REAL MONEY

FIRST EDITION

MARCO CHU KWAN CHING

This publication is designed to provide competent and reliable information regarding the subject matter covered. However, it is sold with the understanding that the author and the publisher are not engaged in rendering legal, financial, or other professional advice. Law and practices often vary from state to state and if legal or other expert assistance is required, the service or a professional should be sought. The author and publisher specifically disclaim any liability that is incurred from the use or application of the content of this book.

ISBN: 978-0-9875292-9-9

"To my parents and my grandparents, who always listen, encourage and instilled me with good spirit"

"To Michael, Frank, Milind and Mark who give me recognitions"

"To many authors who have previously grappled similar topics, without their mentor, this book would not be possible"

- Marco

Acknowledgements

Where do I begin thanking all the people who helped to make this book possible? This book represents one of my most dedicated missions of my life.

I would like to express my gratitude to my parents, Angela Tsang and Tony Chu, for their encouragement. I would like to give special thanks to Mike Maloney who started me on the road to invest in precious metals; and to Peter Schiff for his unparalleled economic insights; Ron Paul for his diligent politics lectures. I would like to thank my brilliant editor Jan Jackson, my friends Matthew Tsang, Lui Kung, Katherine Li, Stella Yang, Sharon Ki, Mark Cunningham, Nadia Lu, for listening to my ideas and giving me support. I would also like to give a big thank you for silverstackers.com and forum members: Bullion Baron, libertadiac, House, Ozboy, Macros_The_Black, silversardine, longtime silver believer, Black_Sun, Water&Food, bullionfrog, hotel 46, RhythmDoctor,hiho, bloomst, Rad Dood, Silverlicious, Dabloodymess, TreasureHunter, valuecreator, XB, renovator, Scott McG, GBN, Aengrod, salty lemon, grinners, Fykus for their passions, enthusiasm and interests in my work. I especially like to thank my grandparents, as my childhood with them is instrumental in bringing this book to fruition.

Contents

Introduction

Introduction

Why did I Write This Book?

Does the world really need another book on money? I struggled a lot before I began. The subject itself is complex and there is no shortage of writers. Yet, many of these books are either too technical or subjective. They are good but might not be accessible to a lot of people. I wish to make a difference.

This book is a journey on real money. It is the single most important subject in life but never taught in school. My work here will fill that gap. This book has eight lessons about money. Before you begin, a word of caution that these lessons will defy a lot of your first beliefs on money and traditional wisdom. So, please be prepared to open to these ideas, they explain the root causes of the problems from the global economy down to your personal finance level. Knowing these can help you to make plans ahead, so you will not be reactionary to forthcoming opportunities. If you use this knowledge wisely, it may potentially create great wealth. We are living in a time of changes in the 21st century. The nature of our money has changed, so should your philosophy. Picking up this book is a sign of change. It is like what Charles Dickens said: *It is the best of times; it is the worst of time*. By following through this book, you will discover silver linings that lead you to prosperity yet invisible to many.

How Important is Monetary Education?

We spend most of our life to earn and spend. Whether we are selling our labor, a product or investing, everything we do involves money. Many people spend time trying to earn more of it, yet few really spend time to understand it.

As more and more middle classes fall below the poverty line, many of us feel like we are going backwards in life. Some may choose to accept it. Some choose to ignore it. Some choose to go back to school in pursuit of higher wages. Some choose to climb the corporate ladder and others choose to jump from job to job. Ironically, all paths will only lead to circles in the long run. Are you one of them? Earning more money cannot solve your money problem. It is merely treating the symptoms rather than curing the disease. Solving a money problem with a higher pay check is a dying trend accelerated by the global economic downturn. Are you puzzled already? Don't worry. There are much better ways than that. But first you must be armed with the right knowledge. If a person is heading down the wrong path financially, it doesn't need academic education to speed him up, it needs monetary education to turn him around.

Can a Pay Rise Solve Your Financial Problems?

"When will I have my pay rise!"

Most companies have a common practice of annual salary review. The idea is to keep staff salaries in pace with the consumer price index (CPI). It is important to most employees. Over the years, it evolved to become more like a curse of addiction, people became dependent on it or took it for granted. Whenever there is a delay in pay adjustments, employees complain and struggle. Company morale falls. Interestingly though, even those people who got an annual pay rise continue to have the same problem the following year, repeating the same phrase like a parrot.

"When will I have my pay rise!"

Can a Higher Professional Education Level Solve Financial Problems?

Over the years, I heard a lot of comments about education and money.

"I have three master degrees and studying for the fourth one, why am I still unemployed?"

"Why is my pay so low? I am a qualified CPA accountant. What else do I lack?"

"I need to go back to school, otherwise I cannot get a higher paid job."

I am also a believer of university education. I see it as a gift from my parents. That's how I am sufficiently literate enough to write this book. I think that getting more professional education is a great way to improve skills, but not necessarily to guarantee a bigger paycheck. It is not a law of return. As more people achieve higher and higher qualifications, studying for a better pay becomes an obsolete idea in the 21st century.

Lifecycle of the Middle Classes

When we were young, remember how our parents used to teach us to *study hard, get a decent job, save money, and contribute back to our society*? I recalled, back in my old university days, students reckoned a high distinction (HD) was as good as gold. It made one feel so good because a HD grade distincted one from the average. To me, the definition of HD never makes any sense, since a Fail (F) grade also highly distincts one from the average. Anyway, to most students, HD grades appear to be tickets to easy street for employment. Do you feel the same? It makes you think the future is going to be bright. If you are in high school, getting a HD average is the same as when you get straight 'A' in your report card.

To finance a university degree, some of us get support from parents, whilst others borrow from the government. Like most McDonald meals, university tuition fees rises. That makes university education becomes unaffordable for people. Government, for good intentions, then tries to increase the borrowing limit to make education more affordable. If you have ever asked older generations about their tuition fees, you will be amazed how cheap it was back then. A part time job was enough to support their entire university education. This is a miracle if you can do that without scholarship or government funding today. If you can do that, you are like an alien from outer space. Ironically though, these university debts accumulated are difficult to be repaid even with a job. So most borrowers are stuck with student loans for years after years. *University debt is the first trap which most pre-middle class incurs.*

For most graduates, the first instinct after graduation is to look for a high paying job. It is almost like a neural reflex action in frogs. Sooner or later, many find out this is not the case.

"But doesn't studying hard mean a ticket for a decent job?" This is the first philosophical shock to most graduates. This is what creates contradictions to their traditional belief. Study hard to get a decent job makes very little sense to me. Some people do not study hard then get a decent job, whereas others study very hard but end up with a job that is not decent. The word "decent" means making more money. Does this relationship always hold? To me, study hard means getting more and more professional at your area of expertise only. An HD in school is not the same as an HD in money.

If you are currently looking for a job, and if you envy those who have decent ones, then please believe me, it doesn't mean that their financial lives are better. Have you wondered why a job is called a "job"? There are good reasons for that. JOB means "Just Over Broke". I love my job, not because of money, but I appreciate how the business system works together, which later on provides me visions to build different assets. Work to learn not to earn. While for many people, a pay day is like a feeding time in a zoo. You can imagine a pay check as a cheesecake and a bonus as a dessert. Do not get addicted to pay checks, pay rise or bonus. Your time is a more valuable asset than money. If you think about it, income tax is one of the largest expenses in life. In most countries, the more you get paid, the more you need to split with the government. That means the government could potentially tax away half of your cheesecake. Through the lens of an income statement, you can see the pattern of a high paying job will drive you nowhere in life. Worst of all, pay checks are addictive. The higher you get paid, the more you will be dependent on it. *The mentality of looking for a high paying job is the second trap which middle class incurs.*

Most middle class do not really realize this until they buy their first dream house. In a famous book *"Rich Dad Poor Dad"* by Robert Kiyosaki with Sharon L Lechter, it points out a house is not an asset. An asset is something which put money into your pocket, whereas a liability is what drives money out of your pocket. I can't agree more. If the house you buy cannot put money into your pocket, that means it is eating the remaining half of your cheesecake. *This is a third trap middle class incurs.*

After tax and mortgage repayment for the house, your cheesecake is down to only one-quarter of the original. This is already an optimistic assumption. Most high paid middle class would argue stubbornly "It is okay, I need to make a living." However, the government doesn't think so. The government thinks our saving rate is too low. Most, if not all, developed countries, starting from U.S., introduce a compulsory retirement plan called 401(K) or superannuation in Australia. The benefit of putting money in a retirement plan is due to tax benefit. But there is one problem. You are allowed to withdraw money in your retirement plan only when you retire. The government is right in the way they reckon our saving rate is too low. But the point is, the rate is too low not because we are not saving, but because there isn't much to save. In the context of retirement plan, they use the word contribute. In dictionary, contribute has several meanings, one is for a charitable purpose. So, if you translate this into plain English, a retirement plan is compulsory for a charitable purpose. Now the cheesecake is less than a quarter. *This is the fourth trap middle class incurs.*

With the remaining fraction of the cheesecake, we can either save it up, consume it, or invest it. If you save it up, put it in a bank and earn an annual interest, by year end you will find out something spectacular. The same dollar you put inside the bank plus interest will buy you less things in general than a year ago. Yes, less things! Why are we encouraged to save money? Don't ask me as I still cannot find a reasonable reason for that. The second option is to spend it. We are born a genius of that. Most companies nowadays encourage us to finance our spending instead of buying it. "Just use it now, you can pay back with interest later". *This is what I called a luxury trap, the fifth trap and the deadliest of all traps.* "So you mean I shouldn't buy anything? What is the point of earning money if I cannot spend it?" Spending is a choice. In the past, you spend what you earn. Today you can spend more than you earn. Some people I knew told me they are struggling financially but at the same time driving sport cars, collecting Prada, and financing their iPhone. *Materialistic is the sixth trap of a middle class.* "So you don't recommend saving, you don't recommend unnecessary spending? What else can we do with our money?" My typical answer will be "Educate yourself then invest it". We will focus on it in the later part of the book.

When reaching the retirement age, comes of the worst nightmare for middle class. Previously, the normal retirement age for a middle class was 65 years old. In U.S., they have gradually increased it to 67. This means, in some cases, you must reach the age of 67 before you can take money out of your retirement account without reduced benefits. Will this retirement age requirement continue to increase? My take is more than likely. Retirement account is only favourable to those who are about to retire. Retirement completes the lifecycle of a middle class. So if you do the maths to add the remaining cheesecakes to your projected retirement account, this amounts will tell you a story. Those who follow this path right from the beginning and play out the middle class scripts exactly like what I described will struggle for retirement.

The Plan for a Two Class Society

If you pause for a moment and connect the dots together, do you feel it is more like a script? Do you feel any coherency? Do you feel that there are some invisible forces steering you to walk in this direction? We never question why. We were programmed and seeded that it is the right thing to do. So we mentally feel right but achieve the exact opposite result. I know you may disagree with me in the first instance, but that little voice inside you tells you that there are some degrees of truth to that statement. But what is that force? Is it our traditions and belief of the society? I doubt it.

Ironically though, it is not difficult to find out what constitutes that force. We are rapidly approaching a two class society: the ultra-rich and the poor. Why the ultra-rich but not the rich? The Ultra-rich is not a person like Bill Gates or Li Ka Sing. Even they are publicly known billionaires in Forbes, they are not the ones I am referring to. The Ultra-rich exist in a group; they exist as a cartel structure. They exist as a social class of their own. A lot of those so called "right things to do" philosophies we believe in today were planted by them long ago before we exist. In a sense, they control the rich. The purpose of this structure is to transfer the wealth from 99% of the population indirectly to them willingly and legally. The ultimate plan is a two class society and a world government. The theme of the Corruption of Real Money is to disclose this complex formula in a way you can understand, capitalize and play their game from outside the system. If you have paid attention to world event, Occupy Wall

Street is just the beginning. Now you know I am not talking about science fiction. Income polarization will only become more and more serious. My question is, do you want to join the crowd protesting, or do you want to be the class to watch the protest? The choice is up to you.

Can I Change My Class?

If you have this thinking, congratulations! This is a great start! This means you have the motivation to fight back and defy the corruption of real money. Don't underestimate this fire. This is the most important step. Yes, you can change your class if you wish. But for things to change, you have to change. Many people hope for the government to change, the tax laws to change, the company to change, the economy to change and the boss to change. But this is impossible, because for these things to change- you have to change! Then the first thing to change is YOUR philosophy about money.

Who is This Book For?

This book is written for individuals who want to revolutionize their lives, by learning about money philosophy and taking actions on it. If you are picking up this book, you might fall into one of these categories:

1. People who are unemployed and have lost direction.
2. People who are working hard on a job but stuck in life.
3. Students who are studying, who are yet to find a true reason for it.
4. Investors who lost much of their wealth during the financial crisis.
5. People who want to study about money.
6. People who are puzzled about what is going on in the economy.
7. People who would like to criticize my book.
8. Politicians who really like helping people.

Part One: The first part of this book is divided into eight lessons. These eight lessons are what constitute the corruption of real money. Please be prepared that this part will drastically change your thinking about money, our government and how our economy works. With this knowledge, you will develop your own crystal ball about which way our global economy is heading and how to profit from it. So be prepared to accept new concepts that might be contradictory to your initial thoughts.

Part Two: To defy the corruption of real money, you need to have flexible plans, executed with the appropriate philosophy and attitude. The second part of this book guides you how to plan ahead. In the real world, different people will have different plans. But all plans from this part are developed from the same framework. The framework to guide you to your financial freedom.

WELCOME TO THE CORRUPTION OF REAL MONEY.

PART I

THE CORRUPTION OF REAL MONEY

Chapter 1

The Root of All Evil

"Grandad, can you show me your treasure?"

"One last time. Will you promise?" Grandad whispered and carried me
to his hidden safe. It was a huge shiny aluminum box that weighed at least
40 kilograms, wall mounted and camouflaged by a framed picture of his
wedding photo.

"Ching Ching, what is the password?" Grandad tried to test my memory.
I am his first grandson, that is why he loves me most. My birthday is
always his primary choice for a password. I was at the age of 8 and had
lived with my grandparents since I was born. That's why I had a very
close relationship with them. My Grandad was a very rich and powerful
person in town. Everyone knew him. Surprisingly, all his sons, lived a
very middle class life. My mom told me that Grandad used to keep his
talents to himself only but never passed them on.

"2812." I pressed the code and unlocked the panel of the safe. Even
under the dim light, the beauty of the treasure shined like the sun.
Grandad took out two $100 banknotes from his pocket and a gold coin
with a $50 dollar face value from his safe.

"Ching Ching, tonight I am going to give you a present. Make a
choice. Which one will you choose?"

I was very young back then. I did not know what a gold coin was. I
had never seen a $100 dollar banknote in my life either. The largest face

value I ever used was $10. Back then $10 was already a lot of money to a kid. With $200 dollar, I could have bought up all the paper games I could not afford at the grocery store. I could even invite the girl next class out for breakfast for the whole semester. Then I looked back at the gold coin and thought. Hang on. But why did Grandad asked me to choose? There must be a reason. I hesitated.

Grandad took out another $100. My temptation grew. Emotions were driving me over logics. Do you know what $300 means for an 8 years old? It would have made me the richest kid in my class! I could even afford to buy a remote controlled helicopter. One for me and one for her. Greed was taking over me.

"How about this?" A few minutes later my Grandad took out a brown $500 banknote out. Surprisingly, this time I grew silence instead. It didn't make sense. This amount was too big and ridiculous for me. My temptation of money suddenly disappeared. Looking at Grandad's vault, I made my choice.

"Grandad, I will have the Gold coin."

"Very good. We have the same synergy" Grandad laughed. "Many people only focus on its price, not many will understand its value and role. This coin is real money. It is money made by gods. I foresee some big economic changes are going to happen in the not too distant future. That's why I will keep saving in gold. Anyway Ching Ching, Happy Birthday."

I was too young to understand what he said. But the wisdom behind these words were so incredible that I carry with me even today.

Mindset of Poverty

The next morning I met up with my best friends David and Billy for cycling. David and I had a lot in common. We both loved cycling, we both wanted to get rich, we both had similar goals, we were both born into a middle class family, and we both did poorly in school. Billy, on the other hand, was from a poor family but did exceptionally well in school. He was our suggested solution in classes.

During our ride, we always passed by a small town. It was the most unpleasant experience during the whole journey. The town was dirty, buildings looked old with high population density, people looked uncivilized and tattooed. A lot of full time beggars were around. However disgusted we felt about this place, every time we passed by, each of us will give 5 cents to a beggar called Paul. Paul was a sad story. He lost his whole family during the Japanese invasion and migrated all the way to Hong Kong. Without education or family, we had shown our sympathy to him.

"Paul. Why are you sitting in here all day? Have you found a job yet?"

"I tried...but there is no use, they won't want me...I have no skills, no money, no family. No future. Nobody wants me. So I must be a full time beggar."

"Doesn't the government help you ?" I asked.

Paul turned his head around and pointed at the small unit inside the old building that we barely even see.

"All my social security paychecks were used to pay rent."

"Why don't you go back to school to acquire skills?"

"You are too fortunate to understand me. I am 46 years old. I am out of time."

All three of us went silence as we continued our way. Even we didn't speak. We knew what we had in mind. We definitely don't want to end up like Paul. He was living in sceptic and shadow every day. Suddenly the advises of our parents flashbacked in our mind. Study hard. Get good grades. Get a decent job.

After a long ride, it was almost dawn. We could see the sun began to set on the horizon. It was a beautiful scene. As usual, we arrived at our ice-cream store and began to enjoy ourselves.

"What do you think of Paul?" I started.

"He needs a job" David agreed.

"So a job can solve money problems?" I sounded sceptical because from memory, my grandad never seems to have a job.

"Of course. That's why my parents don't have Paul's problems. They were both high paid doctors. If you don't mind, come over to my place tonight."

Knowing that it was still our school break, we all agreed for a visit.

Mindset of Middle Class

David's home was a 29 stories high rise apartment. He was living at the top floor. David's parents were both doctors. They worked long hours. They had a maid called Lisa who was employed to take care of all their housework.

"We're home." David put down his keys as he led us into his home. Not surprisingly, no one was home. His parents were obviously not back yet. Lisa was probably shopping for dinner as usual. The interior of David's home was classic. It was two stories high connected by a spiral stairs. The large crystal lamp hanging from the ceiling illuminated the whole sitting room. Above all, it had beautiful water views at the front and mountains at the back. It was incredible.

"Let's go up!" David gestured us as we followed him upstairs.

It was almost 9 o'clock at night. We heard voices from far away approaching from the lift. The conversation got louder and louder, and all three of us lean on the wall and began to eavesdrop. It was David's neighbor.

"Is Vicky still mad at me because I missed her birthday?"

"I am pretty mad at myself... you know...Elaine. I promised you everything, this home. For more than five years, we pray for a child, and when Vicky comes along. Our life seemed complete."

"I understand sweetheart, you did your best. All these years, you put your energy focusing on providing a home and lifestyle to all of us. But your job ... while it did provide a living, it never seems to provide a life... You work so hard to live where we want to live that you don't actually get to live there...and..."

"I will try my best. But how much savings do we have now?"

"Not much...but Everything will be fine...everything is going to be okay. We have been through tough times before..."

"I'm 46 Elaine. A 46 years old executive will not be hired anyway except in McDonald. I am out of time. We are one month behind with our mortgage repayments. Jenny's school fees are due soon. Our car loans are due soon. Our school loan hasn't been paid off. We don't have any money any more sweetheart. I don't know where else to borrow from anymore. We haven't been through this before..."

"So what shall we do?"

"I have no idea. I am sorry my dear.... I promise you everything, and now I provide nothing."

Mr. Chan's family were no strangers to us. Mr. Chan was a top financial analyst in Wall Street. He earned his degree in one of the top 10 universities in U.S. He returned back from U.S. many years ago. Last time Jenny invited David and I into her place, we could see framed certifications hanging all over the walls. We could tell Mr. Chan really feel proud of his qualifications and definitely respect education. These achievements are a symbol of his success. Mrs. Chan, on the other hand, was a popular movie Star. She was gorgeous even in the eye of an 8 year old kid. Sometimes we could even see her in late night dramas on T.V. We once made a joke on Jenny that we saw her mom more than we saw ours. If you ask me to compare, I would say Mr. Chan's family was never below, if not better than David's family. However, our mind changed that night after their conversation. I wondered how many middle class families had the same fate. But at this moment I just wish it wasn't mine. I decided to seek some wisdom from grandad.

So Much for Traditional wisdoms...

"Grandad, how do you solve poverty?"

"Why are you interested in it?" Grandad put down the morning paper.

"Because my friend Paul was living in poverty, no matter how many times we give him money, the next time we see him, he is still the same. He is still living in a mess. Even with government support, he can barely rent that dirty old corner that no human would want to live. With no jobs, no skills, no education, he has no life."

"What does your mom usually tell you when you see people like Paul on the street?"

"My mom tells me to study hard, get good grades, then get a decent job. So in the future I don't end up like Paul begging on the street."

Grandad poured some tea into my cup as I continued my story.

"But Grandad, I don't think this philosophy is entirely right. In fact, Mr. Chan, David's neighbor, who is multiple times wealthier but is suffering the same money problem as Paul…in a much bigger scale…"

"You eavesdropped." Grandad smiled as he placed another prawn dumpling on my plate.

"Ching, do you still remember Robin Hood and his Merry Men?"

"Yes. Rob the rich and give it to the poor." I exclaimed as I was following this cartoon series.

"Exactly. Robin Hood believed poverty can be solved by robbing from the rich and giving it to the poor. Do you know in real life Robin Hood really exists? But of course they were not wearing Lincoln green anymore."

"Really! Show me. Show me." I exclaimed.

"They are our government. Tax the rich and give it to the poor."

"What are taxes? " I ask curiously.

"Do you remember your own piggy account? Well, in real life everyone has a piggy account. At your age, when you earn money, you spend it then put the rest into the piggy account. As you grow older, then the more money you earn, the government will take a slice of your income before you can have the rest. This is called tax - like the government's income."

"What are taxes for?"

"For building roads and bridges, creating jobs, providing housing and providing social security for people like your friend Paul etc."

"Fair enough." I nodded.

"But the problem as a middle class citizen is that the more income you earn, the higher the tax you pay. Assume Mr. Chan's income stream is only his job. Then the harder he works, the more he needs to pay taxes. Income tax can be as high as 50% in some countries."

"So the government is essentially punishing people who work hard?" I began to sense something. "How come Mr. Chan still works so hard? He is an intelligent guy. He got so many certifications framed in his house. How come he didn't know this? Didn't he learn it in school?"

"Different people, different philosophy. If you look around the restaurant, you will see different people from different walks of life. Some are like Paul who let life push them around and don't know how to fight back, some fight back by believing working very hard physically can keep them out of poverty. Some believe in traditional wisdom like study hard and certificates can lead them to great wealth. It is sarcastic to see why everyone is earning money every day, but few would spend time to understand what they are earning."

"But isn't study hard and working hard a good thing to do?"

"Yes. They are virtuous characteristics indeed. But it depends on what you are working hard and studying hard on in life. If you are working hard on studying engineering, you will be an engineering professional. If you work hard on studying accounting, you will be an accounting professional. If you work hard on practicing begging, you will be a beggar professional."

Grandad kept on continuing his lists as I interrupted.

"If I work hard on studying money, I will be a money professional."

"Exactly." Grandad smiled.

I respect my Grandad because he is an influential man. He is also an educator. Unlike traditional teaching, Grandad never pushed me to follow his advice. Quite the opposite, he uses stories and questions to inspire me to think more. Ironically, our school system does quite the opposite. Not many teachers could inspire. Most were working on rushing through syllabus regardless of whether one learns anything. Most of the time, when teachers ask what we don't know, then the class stays quite. It happens in primary school, high school and university. This is not because we know everything already. The sad truth is that most of the time we do not even know what we don't know. That's why I never did well in my primary school. David and I were always sacrificial lambs in the education system.

My Money Professional Journal

Being a professional doesn't mean stop learning. Quite the opposite it simply means the drive to learn more and more. It took me 20 years to understand money and I will continue to be a student of it. Grandad was a terrific mentor in my money professional career. The lessons he taught me were priceless. It opened my eyes to a lot of things others miss or choose to ignore. One of them is time. Time is our most valuable asset, yet many tend to waste it, kill it, spend it rather than invest it. Instead of spending major time on major things, many spend major time on minor things. When you go shopping, I loss count how many people spend countless hours trying to save a few pennies. Yet, when it comes to major things, you will be surprised to see how much time people can afford to spend on it. Well I know this might not apply to everyone, but we cannot deny how much truth there is behind these statements.

Apart from my Grandad's wisdom, I was born with the virtue of reading. After university education, I bought even more books than before. Books are like my mentors. I like to invest my time to learn more not less. Sometimes, I can spend countless hours staying in bookstores. One of my favorite book is Napoleon Hill's *Think and Grow Rich*. I strongly recommend it. It changes your philosophy. Sometimes I am surprised to see people cling to their belief that work hard and study hard can make one rich. Yet it is shameful during my 20 years of book hunting career, I failed miserably to find one single book titled Work Hard and Grow Rich or Study Hard and Grow Rich.

At the present age of 28 years old, I might be too green to have many waves of up and down in terms of life experience in money to share. However from my own four years of research and humble experience of investing, my education paid off. I made my first million (i.e. HKD) at age 25 by investing in real money. One might think this is luck. To me, it is where preparations meet opportunities. I capitalized on it based on financial education. Education on the history of money. Education on finance.

Education on how the global economy works. This book summarized what I learnt to make my luck. I truly believe if I can do it. You can do it.

There is a famous quote from John Rohn: If someone is going down the wrong road, he doesn't need motivation to speed him up. What he needs is the right type of education to turn him around. The following chapters show eight lessons you must know to turn your money philosophy around so that you can capitalize on what is happening with our money today.

Chapter 2

The Game You are Playing

"If you understand how the world financial system works. You know the game you are playing. If you don't know the game and the rules you are playing by, you are going to get slaughtered."

-Michael Maloney. Founder of GoldSilver.com

"Ching, if you ask an individual banker whether he is creating money, he looks at you as if you are mad. He will say of course not! I am not creating money. All I did is that I am accepting deposits from my customers. I put a little of that money as a reserve and lent the rest out. I have not created money. But from my point of view, it is very different. Now come with me. This is your very first lesson about money. Learning how to see things from the lens of a bank."

Do You Prefer to Open a Bank Account or Open a Bank?

It was my first time to accompany Grandad to a bank. I was surprised how polite the staff were to him. Almost everyone recognized him. A lady in customer services even made a ninety degree bow to him as he walked in. Then another lady led us into a room. I wondered how much money Grandad had inside this bank.

"Welcome Wilson. A third deal in a week?" A banker sat in an executive chair greeted us as we entered into his office. The banker looked like a snake oil salesman. I had little trust in him at first sight. My grandad discussed his daily business first as usual then introduced me.

"My grandson. Marco. He is 10 years old. He wants to open a bank account. But before that happens. He wants to learn something about the banks."

"Sure. What do you want to know about the banks?"

"What are banks for?"

"To make money."

"For the customers?"

"Mainly for the banks…"

"But why doesn't the bank advertisement mention this?"

My grandad chuckled. But he didn't interfere our conversation.

"Usually it is already implied in the banking reserve we made."

"How much is that?"

"About $250,000,000 in reserve," The banker rolled his eyeballs.

"Wow...Do you make it out of the customers?"

"Yes. Customers just like your grandad." The banker smiled.

"How many assets does the bank has?"

"About $1,000,000,000."

"Did the bank make that amount too?"

"No. This is the money the bank used to make money."

"I see. But did the bank keep the money in a safe?"

"No. Not at all. We lent it to our customers."

"But if the money is lent out, then the bank does not have the money…"

"No, we haven't had it."

"If the bank doesn't have the money, how is it asset?"

"Oh…We manage it as if we would make it back after we lent it out. So it is okay."

"But the money must be somewhere…" I felt puzzled.

"Yes, So we call this $1,000,000,000 our liabilities."

"But why is the bank liable for the $1,000,000,000?"

"Because these money does not belong to the bank."

"Then why does the bank has the money?"

"It had been lent by the customers when they put money into their bank account. It is really lending money to the bank. That's why we pay people interests." "What do the bank do with that money?"

"We lent it to other customers."

Even more puzzled. "But you just said money they lent to other people was assets. Then Assets and Liabilities are the same thing"

Grandad chuckled again.

"You can't really say that." The banker shook his head.

"But you have just said it. Say, for example, if I put $100 in my account. The bank is liable to pay me back. Right? So it is banks' liabilities." The banker nodded his head.

"But when the bank lent it to someone like my grandad, then he is liable to pay it back to the bank. So it is an asset in the banks' balance sheet. It is the same $100. Don't you agree?" I continued.

"Yes...But..."

"Then it cancels out. The bank didn't make any money at all."

"Theoretically..."

"But if the bank isn't making any money. Where about does the bank get the $250,00,000 in reserve?"

"I have told you already. This is the money the bank made."

"But how?"

"Well, when the bank lent your $100 to someone, it charges him interest."

"How much?"

"Depends on the Bank rate. Sometimes 5% or 6%. That's our profits."

"But when I lent the bank money. Do I charge the bank interest as well?"

"Yes you do."

"How much interest can I charge?"

"Half a percent."

Grandad chuckled again.

"But it is only if you don't draw the money out again." The banker added.

"Oh my goodness. Of course, I am going to draw the money out again. If I don't draw it out again. Why wouldn't I keep it under my mattress instead?"

"But the bank doesn't like you to draw the money out again."

"But why? I am helping the bank to reduce their liabilities. Don't they like to reduce their liabilities?"

"No. Because if you remove it. Then they cannot lend it out to other people."

"But if I want to draw It out. I can do that. Can't I?"

"Certainly."

"But suppose the bank had already lent out my money to another customer. Then what happen if I want my money back?"

"The bank will then let you have another customer's money."

"But suppose if that customer wants to have his money bank too…then will the bank let me have his money?"

I could tell Grandad was trying terribly hard to control his laughter.

"Hey kid. You are purposely being obtuse." The banker's face turned red.

"No, I am being accurate. If everyone wants their money all at once…"

"This will never happen in banking practice" The banker interrupted.

"Well … I suppose that's all I wanted to know. Mr. banker. Can you think of anything you can tell me?"

"Now you can open a bank account."

"Just one last question."

"Sure."

"Wouldn't I be better off if I go and open a bank?"

How Money is Created in the Bank?

"It is well enough that people of the nation do not understand our banking and monetary system, for if they did, I believe there would be a revolution before tomorrow morning"

-Henry Ford

"If you want to understand why our money is corrupted, first you must understand how money is created in the banks." I heard that thousands of times from my Grandad.

Suppose you arrive at a town called *ForeverTown*, and prior to your arrival, there was no money. You have $1,000, and you want to deposit it into a bank account. The $1,000 will appear in your balance sheet as an asset. An asset in your balance sheet is the money you saved, but it appears in the bank's balance sheet as a liability. In other words, the bank owes you $1,000 as a customer deposit.

Your Balance Sheet

Asset	Liability
$1,000 (Saving)	

Bank's Balance Sheet

Asset	Liability
	$1000 (Customer Deposit)

Now, the bank cannot create money in this way, so it has to loan out part of your saving to those who want to borrow it. The bank knows that you will take out part of your deposits, but it also knows that there is a rare chance you will take out all of your deposits either. So the bank can loan out part of your deposits.

Since the federal rule says that the bank can only loan up to 90% of the customer deposit, (i.e. $900), and will keep the remaining 10% deposit as a reserve (i.e. $100). The bank is said to make a 10% reserve ratio. Pretty simple. Right?

Suppose now the Bank lends $900 to Billy to buy an engagement ring for his girlfriend from Mary's Swarovski Shop. The money is now transferred to Mary's Bank Account which looks like this.

Mary's Balance Sheet

Asset	Liability
$900 (Saving)	

Bank's Balance Sheet

Asset	Liability
	$900 (Customer Deposit)

Logically, your saving deposit will reduce to $100 after the bank loan out 90% of your deposit. Robbery! Let's have a second look at your balance sheet at this point.

Your Balance Sheet

Asset	Liability
$1000 (Saving)	

Bank's Balance Sheet

Asset	Liability
	$1000 (Customer Deposit)

Your deposits are still in your account. Untouched. So the size of the economy in *ForeverTown* is now $1,900 instead of $1,000. ($1000 from your deposits plus $900 from Mary's deposits).

[**Note**: This is just an example. In reality if you tell your banker you want to loan money to buy an engagement ring, the chances are pretty rare except using your credit card. Bank loans money to people to buy properties, or a business start up.]

Now, with the new deposit of Mary. The bank can once again loan it out at a 10% reserve ratio. The newly created money will be $810 ($900 x 0.9). If this process repeats, you will eventually find out that under a 10% ratio $10,000 sprang into existence. ($9,000 in loan and $1,000 in deposit). Is that real? Yes, it is very real. It happens every day. If you ever wonder why today's money supply is multiplied many times since your grandparents' time; if you ever wonder why everything cost so much today. That's it. This is one part of the mystery. It is called fractional reserve banking.

Lesson 1:
Money (currency) today is loan into existence.

Average people work hard and save. That blood and sweat of labor is what creates value in money. Yet the gap between how banks create money out of thin air and the effort to earn is so enormous that no wonder Henry Ford thought there would be a revolution tomorrow morning if people actually discovered how the banking system works.

Who gives the Banks the Right to Create New Money?

When you or I print money and use it, this is called counterfeiting, which is illegal, and for this crime we get locked up in jail. But isn't fractional reserve banking doing the exact same thing? What gives banks the right to bring new money into existence?

The answer is people.

A bank cannot loan money without our permissions. When a person buys a house and needs to take out a loan, a contract is signed to borrow money from the bank. This signature gives the banks the right to create money.

How Come Everything is So Expensive!

When you and I work hard to earn a salary or create jobs, what makes our earned money valuable is the labor, talent, ideas, time and effort we put into our jobs. Our blood and sweat are what creates the value. Each unit of currency has a unit of value representing people's hard work. But fractional reserve banking system is like smoke and mirrors because what it is doing is diluting or stealing the value of each unit of currency from the people. It borrows prosperity from the future. To make it simple, let's say the first $1,000 you bring over the *ForeverTown* has a purchasing power of 1,000 units of apples. If we assume there is a fixed supply of apples, then the price of one apple will cost exactly $1.(i.e. Total number of apples divided by the total amount of currencies). When the bank lends out part of your savings ($900) and keeps a fraction ($100) as a reserve, by the time this $900 entered our economy, was spent and deposited into someone's bank account, *ForeverTown* would have $1,900 chasing 1,000 units of apples. Many people will feel that the price of apples went up from $1 to $1.9 and wonder what happens. As this process continues, the currency supply will reach $10,000, and under a 10% reserve ratio, the price of one apple will jump to $10! Do you have this feeling today? Everyone is pointing a finger at greedy businessmen, yet businesses are also victims of the rising price. The expansion of the money supply is called inflation, rising price of apples is the result of inflation.

Is fractional reserve banking legal? I leave this for you to decide for yourself. It is ironic that when a person loses $1,000 in his bank account, he will spend major time on getting it back. However, when we lose $1,000 due to inflation, many people don't care or even realize it. Those who sense it just talk about it then forget it. Few will ask what to do about it.

Knowing What Banks Think

When I was little, I was always puzzled why grandad was so popular with banks, but it makes more sense as I gain his wisdom in seeing things through the eyes of elite bankers.

"Like most people, if you think the banks really want you to deposit your money in it and earn interest, you do not really understand how banks think."

"What do you mean? Isn't that what everyone is doing? Don't banks need your money so that they can lend it out?"

"In a sense, yes and no. The bank does not need a lot of customers' deposits to loan them out. For banks to make money, all they need are people to loan money continuously. The bigger the amount they loan out, then the more loans they made. The more loan interest they collect, then the more profitable they become."

Further on from our example on *ForeverTown*, the reason why Grandad says banks do not need a lot of customer deposits is because the first $1,000 you deposit in the bank is the only money the bank actually need to create the other $9,000 out of thin air through fractional reserve banking. Most of the money the bank lent out is nothing but a bookkeeping entry. So if, you think about it clearly, the only transaction makes economic sense is the interest charged on the first $1,000 deposits. Charging interest on the remaining $9,000 is like charging money created out of nothing. Isn't this a David Copperfield magic? Ironically, this process continues every day, but concealed even from bankers working every day, let alone customers. No one questioned this as long as the correct bank account balance is displayed on the screen.

Over the years, I know alot of people panic when they try to borrow money from the bank to buy a house. It is intimidating to borrow a large sum. But, if you know what a banker thinks, you might think differently. In reality, he is as desperate to loan you money as you need to borrow it! Where on earth can you find deals like that? So if, you know what they think, it gives you an unfair advantage towards those who don't.

Lesson 2:

Banks make huge profits from fractional reserve banking. They want to loan money out so they can collect interest. The faster a bank makes a loan, and the higher the loan amount, the more profitable a bank becomes.

Do Banks Like You to Pay Down the Loan?

Most people will have the impression that banks want you to pay down the loan as quickly as possible so that they can have the money back. Ironically, this is not the case. Banks are not very interested in getting the loan back. They are more interested in knowing whether they can receive regular interest on the loan. If a person pays down the loan, the bank will have to find another person to loan money to. This applies to individual as well as national level.

The Larger the Loan the Safer it is...

Banks are more interested in larger loans. The larger the loan, the better, because it collects more interest. Imagine a loan made from A.B.C Bank to the Indonesian Government netting hundreds of millions of dollars profit, which has the same effect of loaning money to Mary who took out a mortgage to buy a house. The bank will definitely go for a bigger loan.

But isn't loaning out a huge sum of money involves higher risk? What if the other party defaults? In reality, the larger the loan, the safer it is. Although this is against traditional thinking, it holds a lot of truth. Remember banks profits from the interest payment, in other words, the interest payments are what banks want. If the loan is big enough, the bank will be unlikely to let you fail. Because if you default, the bank will lose its profits. So the bank would rather lend you even more money in order to cover your existing bad debt so that they can continue to collect their profits. Crazy isn't it? In some cases, if the loan is so massive that it involves hundreds of million of dollars, the government will step in and bailout.

You Do Not Really Need Weapons to Conquer Countries Today

In 2011, the World Bank had loaned a total of $43 billions to developing countries. Did they know that some of these poorest countries would not be able to repay the debt? Sure. That was their good intention to help third world countries. On the surface, this argument could make sense. Without the World Bank's support, how could the economy of the poorest countries continue? But if the aide is so helpful, why does the gap between rich and poor countries continue to widen? Why do poor people continue to become poorer? Why is the income polarization so huge compared to half a century ago? It seems like all the slogans to fight poverty have achieved the exact opposite result from that originally intended. The picture below tells you everything about poverty.

World Bank's Balance Sheet			Poor Country's Balance Sheet	
Asset	**Liability**		**Asset**	**Liability**
$9,000,000,000 (Loan to third world countries, 1% interest rate)				$9,000,000,000 (Loan from world bank ,1% interest rate)

What if a poor country cannot pay its interest on the loan? The bank will give them another loan on top to cover the interest repayment. This is called perpetual-debt play. This happens every day to ensure poor countries remains poor and rich countries to remain rich, all in the name of friendly support. It is sarcastic to see poor countries continue to accept this agreement and wonder why they are poor. Poverty cannot be solved by giving people more money. This applies to both individual and national levels. Yesterday, we needed weapons to conquer otherlands. Today it is not necessary at all. Countries can be controlled by controlling their finance, keeping them addicting to this cheap money.

What Happens if Loans Turn Bad...

Have you ever seen long queues in outside banks waiting to withdraw deposits? My grandad had this experience as a kid in 1930. But why did people do that? The answer is the loss of confidence in banks. When people deposit money into banks, they expect their money to be safe. Well, it wasn't the case back then. By the principle of fractional reserve banking, banks usually only kept 10% of the deposits to back the other 90% which they loan out. Banks do not have all the money if everyone demands it back at the same time.

When a borrower cannot repay a loan and has no assets to compensate, then the bank has to write it off as a loss. In this case, the bank will not loan him anymore money because they know he could not repay anyway.

So loaning to small investors is actually positioning a bank at higher risk. As you can see, most of the money (90%) that banks lent out is created out of bookkeeping entry. It costs the bank nothing.

Even though it costs the bank nothing, sometimes book entry loss can be intensely painful as well. When bad debt is written off as an asset to the bank, that bank stops collecting interests, but is still liable for the money it borrows from the depositors. If there is a wave of bad loans hitting the market, depositors' money held by the bank is at risk. When this happens, depositor's confidence in the banks will be shaken. That's why depositors all rush to the bank and withdraw their money. This process is called a bank run. When that happens, banks are likely to fail. In order to prevent this from happening, the banks either need to remove their previous profits or draw out capitals from its stockholders. Both ways are equally painful. However, if this can't even cover all the loss in bad loans, then the game is over. The bank will declare itself insolvent. This is what happened to many banks in the U.S. after the financial crisis in 2008. Many people defaulted on their mortgages when the loans turned bad. From 2008 until today, there are hundreds of banks that failed due to bad loans.

Banking Crisis

If everyone demands their deposit at the same time, a bank will face a shortage of liquidity. When banks do not have sufficient currencies or cash to meet the demand, they are in a liquidity crisis. But as long as the bank assets and loans are sound, they can always borrow from healthy banks, that have sufficient credit. The idea is to restore people's confidence and prevent a bank run.

However if the healthy banks realize that there is no way that troubled banks can pay back all its obligations, and no other banks want to lend them money, depositors must be very careful. The bank is in a solvency crisis. This will trigger bank runs.

My grandad once gave me a very good analogue on the difference between liquidity and insolvency and what happens in a banking crisis.

"Ching, if you have dinner in a restaurant and you don't have enough cash with you in your pocket to pay the bills, you are in a liquidity crisis. You can either borrow money from your friends around you (hopefully they won't charge you interest) or you may always use your credit card. However, if you are unemployed, with no money and huge debts, then you are in a solvency crisis after finishing this dinner." Grandad finished his last piece of steak and began to leave the table.

"Wow. Don't leave! I have no money now." I yelled.

"What crisis are you in now?" Grandad teased.

" Liquidity crisis. But I can use your card."

"Good. You have been listening. By the way, I am just going to the toilet."

"Ching, if a banking crisis happens on one bank (solvency crisis), it is very likely to cause people to bank run on other healthy banks (liquidity crisis). When this happens, all banks will run on low reserves, companies cannot borrow money since banks have no money to lend. The short term interest rate will spike and triggers a lot of other consequences like mortgage defaults; corporation bankrupcy, unemployment etc. In 1907, U.S. banks were facing a liquidity shortage crisis, panic spread throughout the nations, and many local banks and business were forced to declare bankruptcy. New York Exchange fell almost 50% to the previous high. Wall Street was almost wiped out. This was the infamous Panic of 1907. J.P. Morgan being the wealthiest banker in U.S. resolved the crisis by injecting large sums of capital and restored market confidence".

The Federal Reserve (The Fed)

"When I write a check, there must be sufficient funds in our account to cover the check, but when the Federal Reserve writes a check, there is no bank deposit of which that check is drawn. When the Federal Reserve writes a check, it is creating money."

-Putting it simply 1984 – Federal Reserve publication

My grandad was a true scholar. Even at retirement age, he never stopped learning. Never too old to learn was his slogan for young people on a television show. I am very fortunate that I could accompany Grandad during most of my childhood. His hobbies influenced me. Apart from his leisure in drawing Chinese fine art, I found that most of his other leisure time was spent inside his personal library. His library was meticulously designed with a room hidden behind warm wood floor-to-ceiling bookshelves. Somehow I always had the wild imagination that there is a secret room hidden behind the bookshelf, Maybe I had been watching too many cartoons. Grandad had a vast interest in different subjects like economics, history, taxes, money, politics, business, patents, real estates, precious metals, finances, investing, marketing, physics, energy, philosophy, computing and even gambling. Some of his books were thick like dictionaries. He is a professional book collector. I also had my own personal library at the age of 10, but my scale was a lot smaller. My collections were mainly a series of horror novels called Goosebumps by R.L.Stine and Fighting Fantasy from Ian Livingstone. So words like paranormal, creatures, horror could never escape my eyes.

Once, I followed Grandad into his library as usual, I unexpectedly discovered a book which later on changed my entire life. The book title is *The Creature from Jekyll Island* by G. Edward Griffin.

"Grandad, Look! Look! Can I have a look at this one!" I pleaded when I first saw the title. It was a thick one.

"Horror story?" I asked suspiciously.

"Yes. A very scary one indeed. Unlike your horror book collection. This one I got here is non-fiction." Grandad chuckled.

"There is a real creature at the Jekyll Island?" I anticipated a response.

"Yes a real one. Its name is called the Federal Reserve. (The Fed). It eats people alive." Grandad replied.

"Grandad. I considered myself an expert on mythology creatures. I knew about hydras, centaurs, harpies, mummies, medusa, cerberus, but I have never heard anything called the Federal Reserve." I was puzzled.

"I am not surprise you don't know. Not many people even at my age know its existence. Yet it affects us every day, every moment."

"Where is Jekyll Island?" I asked suspiciously.

"It is located in U.S, an island off the coast of the U.S. state of Georgia." Grandad pointed the location on his world map hanging on the wall.

"But U.S. state of Georgia is very far from us. How does this affects us?"

"The creature had slowly evolved throughout the ages. It no longer needs to reach you physically."

"But how? What kind of creature is that? How is it formed?" I became excited.

Bank A   **Bank B**   **Bank C**

"It all began with a secret meeting on Jekyll Island in Georgia, where the Fed is born. The Fed is a banking cartel formed in 1913. Do you still remember the results of Panic of 1907? It was a very important lesson in U.S. banking history. The primary reason for creating the Fed was to prevent banking crisis like this from happening again. The crisis happened not because of a bad economy, but because banks are loan up to a point where they do not have enough reserve to meet the depositor's requirement. So the lesson learnt was that they need a central banking structure to prevent liquidity shortage crisis and acts as the lender of last resort."

"The Federal Reserve is created to fit that role." I responded.

"Exactly." Grandad then drew the banking structure on his whiteboard. The structure had three banks at the bottom and a Federal Reserve on the top.

"Before the Fed was created, if Bank A has a solvency crisis, all depositors would rush to the banks and withdraw their money. Because if they didn't all their hard earned money would vaporize when Bank A collapses. There was no deposit insurance by the government back then. Like all other banks, Bank A also worked on the fractional reserve banking system. When a bank run happens, and it cannot meet the depositor's needs; Bank A will seek help from Bank B and Bank C."

"If Bank B and Bank C have a sufficient loan for Bank A, then the banking crisis might settle down. If not, then Bank A will become insolvent."

"Exactly. A bank run in the Bank A will trigger bank run in Bank B and Bank C even if they are healthy. This is because depositors don't know which banks have problems. Another issue was that the currency supply was inelastic."

"What is the meaning of inelastic currency supply?"

"It means a fixed currency supply. When Bank B and Bank C do not have sufficient cash to loan to Bank A, it might lead to a chain reaction and cause the whole banking system to collapse. It is because there are no excessive money."

I nodded in agreement.

"So what they need is someone who can have the power to inject money to save banks anytime to restore depositors confidence. They need a money supply which can expand and contract at will, they need an elastic money supply."

"But how is that possible? Who can have such a power?"

The Birth of the Creature

Since the Panic of 1907, many rival banks grew and began dominating the market shares. In order to survive, the world leading banking consortia foresaw and decided to join force to eliminate their common enemy-competition. Morgans, Rockefellers, Rothschild, Warburg and Kuhn Loeb were the major players back then. Among them, Morgans and Rockefellers were the focus in U.S. Rothschild and Warburg groups were the focus in Europe.

The meeting at the Jekyll Island was highly secretive. It was organized by six men. Six men travelled thousand of miles to a tiny island. Six men who were estimated to control one-fourtha quater of the world's entire wealth. Nelson W. Aldrich, a very powerful government agency in the Senate, was the host of the event. Aldrich was the father in law of John.D. Rockefeller's son – The son of the first billionaire in the world. If we use Bill Gates' wealth as a reference, John.D. Rockefeller's net worth is roughly about 10 times more than him in today's dollar.

The meeting was held in one of J.P.Morgan's resort in Jekyll Island. Because of the secrecy, the meeting was disguised as a duck hunting event. Guests who attended the meeting came individually and never disclosed their true identity, only their first name. Servants and caretakers were given long term vacations for that period. This was to make sure no one could ever recognize the guests.

Their meeting concluded that previous banking crisis was caused more by banks "loan up" rather than real economic factors. The cause of the crisis was because banks competed recklessly to loan money to maximize their profit. Their reserve rate was close to zero. This reached boiling point when the system became unsustainable and faced an inevitable collapse. The results were that a lot of hatred accumulated against banks after the Panic of 1907. In order to survive, they allied together to form a cartel structure. Six powerful men in a room deciding the fate of the nation's financial future. The entire system can be broken down into plans to achieve the following five agendas.

1. Stop the growing influence of rival banks and ensure that control over national financial resources would remains in the hands of the present.

2. Make money supply elastic in order to reserve the trend of private capital formation and to recapture the industrial loan market.

3. Pool the merger reserve of all nation banks into one large reserve to protect them against bank run.

4. Shift the inevitable loss of the owner of the banks to the taxpayers.

5. Convince the Congress that the scheme was to protect the public.

[**Note**: Congress is part of U.S. government to legislate laws]

Among other objectives, the first objective of stopping rival banks and control over national financial resources were easy. They had sufficient financial capability to make that happens. All that was needed was to prepare technical paperwork and reword vocabularies into legislative phases. The second and third objectives should not be difficult ones either. This was the intended purpose of having this new central system- to make money supply elastic and act as the lender of last resort. But the fourth and fifth ones were the real headache. These were their true objectives, not the government nor the will of the public. How could they shift their inevitable loss to the taxpayers? How could they have Congress convinced they were trying to protect the public?

The True Color

In order to establish the system they were trying to create, a name must be meticulously chosen. Words like "Central", "Cartels" or "Banks" would have them sound defeated already. Back then, the public had just gone through a banking crisis, depositors' loss money, there were a lot of hatred built up against the banking sectors. Not only that, the democratic always shown opposition against centralized bodies. No one would like to hear about central banking system. In order to gain public trust, they needed to use words which disguised themselves as part of the federal government. Only then, they could gain acceptance. That's why the word federal was chosen. One of their primary purposes was to act as the lender of last resort, in the name of being a reserve bank. So the name Federal Reserve was used.

They also need to paint a picture of themselves being regional, not a centralized authority. So before the Federal Reserve Act was passed by the Senate, they must structure the Federal Reserve conservatively at the very beginning to conceal their true color. Aldrich safeguarded the plan by making a brilliant speech.

"The organization is not a bank, but a cooperative union of all banks of the country for a defined purpose"

Two years later the Federal Reserve Act was passed by the Congress. They removed the safeguard.

"The measure reorganizes and adopt principles of a central bank. Indeed, if one works out as the sponsors of the law hope, it will make all incorporated banks joint owner of a central dominating power"

Aldrich was the one who took this task to submit their first drafted plan. But coincidentally due to the Senate illness, the plan was submitted by Frank Vanderlip and Benjamin Strong. This was famously known as *Aldrich Bill*. Aldrich was obviously a team member of the plan, but he claimed to have little to do with it. His intention was to keep himself outside the loop.

When asked about their response about the monopoly of this act, Aldrich intelligently responded.

"The bank I proposed ...An ideal method of fighting monopoly. It would not be possible for itself to become a monopoly and it would prevent other banks from combining monopolies. With an earning limit of 4.5% there could not be monopolies."

To fulfill their last two objectives, they must have public support. But how could they do that? How could they involve the government as an agent to shift the inevitable loss from the bankers to the taxpayers? At the same time, the public buys the theory that the system is trying to protect them. The mechanism works like this: First they induce economic bubbles and wait until it bursts. Public asks for help then they print money or through taxation to bailout large corporations that are too big to fail. I can give you plenty of examples about how this mechanism was used several times in history. But the most recent one we all know is the subprime mortgage crisis in 2008. Before going into that, let's look at how the Federal Reserve creates money.

How the Fed Creates Money?

When you listen to the Fed meeting dozen of times, you probably never find them admitting they are printing money even though they are. Instead, you will find a lot of technical financial terms that only financial gurus might have the knowledge to decode what they are saying.

The Fed creates money through monetary policies. Although these monetary policies are intended to be difficult, they can be simplified as accepting IOUs to create money out of thin air. If you are not really interested in knowing how the Fed creates money, please feel free to skip this part.

[**Note**: I Owe You (IOUs) is a simplified term for Bond. A bond is a promised made to borrow money and pay back later with interest. If the bond is issued by the government, it is a government bond.]

There are three ways how the Fed creates money. The first one is purchasing a bond from the Treasury through Open Market Operation. For simple analogue, think of open market operation as an aution platform like eBay; bonds or securities issued by the Treasury (i.e. Treasury bond) as items for auction.

Treasury Issues a Bond

The Fed Buys the Bond by printing money

[**Note**: Securities are like bonds but with assets attached to it. Home Mortgage is a type of securities for banks because if one fails to pay the mortgage, banks have the right to take back the house].

When the Treasury issues a bond, it is simply a piece of paper with ink on it. What gives it value is the perception of trust by the people. The trust is derived from government's promises to pay back its IOUs through taxation or other means. In the Treasury auction, many organizations or countries participate to buy the bond. The Federal Reserve is only one of the buyers. Now the trick lies here, when other buyers (corporation or countries) purchases the bond, it makes sense as the currency they used for purchase have value in it. The value is derived from everyone's hard work like yours and mine by working nine-five in the society. But when the Federal Reserve buys a bond, there is no money in its account in the first place. All it is doing is running the printing press and print the money out to the government.

Lesson 3:

When the Federal Reserve buys a Bond, it is printing money.

Once the Federal Reserve buys a bond, it deposits a check into the government account. The money is used to finance government expenses and pay government employee. This is the first wave how fiat currency enters the economy. Remember when Federal Reserve buys a bond, it will not affect the economy yet. We will feel inflation when the money find its way into the commercial banks. So buying a bond simply means adding liquidity (i.e. currency) into the money supply. Conversely, selling a bond means withdrawing liquidity from the money supply. This is how the Fed makes the money supply elastic.

The second method is by loaning member's bank through the discount window. Discount window is a common terminology for member banks to get a loan from the Federal Reserve. But why do the banks need loans from the Fed? There are many good reasons for that. One reason is because banks can gain more profit by running on low reserve. Their operating margin is extremely thin from time to time. So if they have trouble meeting the depositor's withdrawals, they will have to remove assets from their balance sheet which lowers their profit. To understand how discount window works, let's look at some maths. Suppose a bank requests a loan from the Fed, say $1,000,000 at a rate of 10% interest. The cost of running this loan will be $100,000 per year.($1,000,000 x 0.1). Like depositors money from the public, banks are allowed to loan this borrowed money from the Fed to the public. Through fractional reserve banking, that bank will have an additional $9,000,000 to lend to its customers. So if that bank lends at a rate of 12% interest, the gross return will become $1,080,000. ($9,000,000 x 0.12). When we subtract this from the running cost of $100,000 from the bank. The bank will have a net return of about $980,000. In other words, the banks borrow $1million from the Fed and can almost have a risk free return within one year of operation. This profit is made on behalf of expanding the money supply of the country. We will see how this swallow us all later.

The third method is by simply changing the reserve ratio. By federal law, all member banks are required to have a reserve ratio of 10%. Well this is what the "reported" figure is. For $1 million, the bank can actually loan up to $9,000,000. Crazy fractional reserve banking. However if the reserve ratio is reduced to 0.1%, you can do the maths. The lower the reserve ratio, the more currency they can create.

Of course, there are other methods the Fed can indirectly create money as well. Trust me, they are exceptionally creative. Another intriguing one is that over time the banks are becoming more and more dependent on the use of time deposits. As you have probably experienced this already, time deposit is a type of deposit where money is not immediately available when you withdraw. In other words, the money in time deposit is loaned out. That's why in banks, the longer the time deposit, the better rate you get. In 1945, time deposit played a very insignificant role compared with demand deposit. By 2007, time deposit became the dominated side of customers' deposits.

The Name of the Game is Bailout

Most of us would have experienced the global financial crisis (GFC) of 2008. It shocked the entire global economy. Even today as I am writing, many businesses are still in the process of recovery. Is the crisis affecting everyone? Yes, definitely. It weakens the job market, the banking sectors, the housing market and the result are monetary policies causing world wide inflation.

While most people will probably agree that 2008 GFC was a random, sudden and independent event. I have a very different perspective. Before the crisis, a few financial experts like Peter Schiff had this event predicted in advance. Politicians like Ron Paul had been warning about this crisis for years. My Grandad did not predict this event. But as a student of the financial crisis, he had been paying close attention to the artificial low interest rates between 2001 to mid 2003 which fuelled the real estate boom in U.S.

But aren't people working at the Federal Reserve honored as the mastermind of finance and economic? Aren't these people graduated at the top universities in the world? That's why they are in charge of the country's money supply. Why couldn't they see the crisis coming while it appears to be so apparent to others?

If we conclude the Fed carelessly missed this crisis. It makes me shiver to see how the five agendas of the Federal Reserve play out perfectly every time before, during and after a financial crisis. To understand how it works, let's travel back in 2008 and briefly revisit when happened in slow motion.

The Federal Reserve years of artificially low interest rate caused the real estate market to boom. This created an illusion to people that real estate price would always rise base on history. Many made fortunes by buying a house, holding it for one year of so, and then sold it for a profit. Banks, on the other hand, began to lend like crazy. They knew that if loans turned bad, the Federal Reserve would bail them out. In the past, when people needed to take out a mortgage, they need down payment and have a good credit rating. Now, the bank is giving it to anyone who wishes to sign the paper. If you look it from a bank's perspective, all they want are loans. The more loans made, the more profits they generate. So the game becomes simple.

Make as many sub-prime loans as possible, then re-package them and send to unsuspicious investors. Two government sponsored corporations: Fannie Mae (Federal National Mortgage Association) and Freddie Mac (Federal Home Loan Mortgage Corporation) are part of the organization for packing these loans- mortgage backed securities (MBS).

But as you know nothing can go up forever. Every bubble pops. When it did, housing prices declined sharply. Foreclosures were everywhere. Banks and investors holding sub-prime mortgages were in trouble. This crisis affected everyone across the board. Since the global economy is highly dependent on one another. If one economy fails, the other will be affected like a house of cards. Back then, many corporations failed and people lost their jobs. Once again as predicted, public cried for help.

It's time. That's when the Federal Reserve stepped in. The total loans guaranteed by Fannie Mae and Freddie Mac in U.S. dollar amounted to $12 Trillions. Over 740,000 homes felt into foreclosure. Immediately, U.S. Treasury approved a bailout package from the Fed and injected a total of $800 billion. This is called Quantitative Easing I. (QE I)

Now the trick is here. Base money is the amount of cash in circulation It measures how many dollars in existence. It took 200 years for U.S., base money starting from the time of Washington D.C up to 2008 September to went from zero to $825 billions. When the Federal Reserve wrote a check to the Treasury to buy back the MBS, the money supply increased to $1.8 trillion. In March 2009 in the following year, the Fed announced another round of quantitative easing amounting to $1.2 trillion. (QE II). So in less than a year, the total money supply in U.S. increased from $825 billion to $3 trillion. Since U.S. dollar is the world reserve currency, when U.S. creates this amount of money, central banks worldwide need to print the same amount of local currency to keep the exchange rate stable. That's the reason why the world is sensing raging inflation.

Everything up to this point is just the beginning of a new financial disaster and more and more bailouts. On the same year of the event, AIG Insurance Co was also bailout by the Federal Reserve by giving them $85 billions. Shortly thereafter, American Express also received $3.39 Billions. General Motors were also allowed to transform its structure to a commercial bank, so it is also eligible for bailout. Bank of America received a $15 Billion bailout, then invest in China's Construction Bank.

Apart from banks, even auto makers claims they have trouble making interest payments on bad loans on MBS they invested in. So the auto industry was given $17.4 Billion.

All this bailout money expanded the money supply and diluted the dollar you and I are holding. As you can see from the pattern here, the astronomical amount of money shifted the loss from banks to the taxpayer's shoulders. This is the meaning of the game - bailout.

A Claim Check for Future Generation

"Ching, remember that there is no such thing as a free lunch in our economy. All the money the Fed and banks created comes with a price tag. Every dollar in existence is a promise to tax us until the day we die. It taxes us through inflation by diluting every dollar we hold. The money loan into existence today is borrowed from the future. From 1913 until today, all the money we hold lost 90% of the purchasing power. That's why future generation will only feel poorer even with a larger account balance."

DOLLAR VALUE

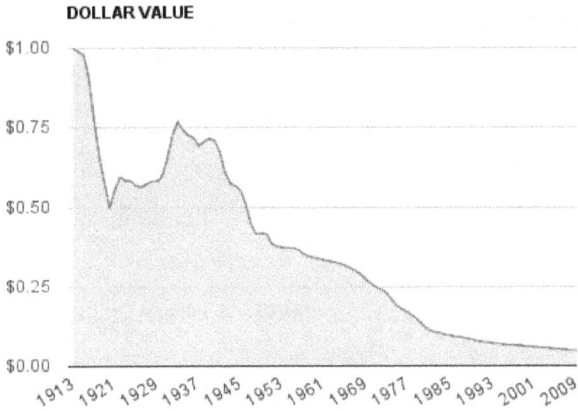

Purchasing Power of the US dollar, January 1913=$1.00

"It is not the amount of money we have which is important but the value of the dollar we are holding."

"You got it."

How the World Financial System Works?

"If you know how the world financial system works, you know the game you are playing. If you don't know the game and the rules you are playing by, you are going to get slaughtered."

Over the years, Grandad had been explaining how the entire financial system works. He explained it was a complex system designed to transfer wealth from the public to the government and the elites. As I grown up, my knowledge increases. Now I am going to show you in 5 steps how these pictures fit together. Are you ready?

Step 1 When the Treasury say I Own You....

When the Treasury wants to raise money, it issues a bond. A bond is nothing but an IOU. It promises to pay interests to the bond holder. The reason why Treasury bond is valuable is only because of trust of government.

Primary dealers like Goldman Sachs, J.P. Morgans shops in the Treasury auction to buy these bonds.

[**Note**: Primary dealers can also be Countries like Australia China and Japan etc.]

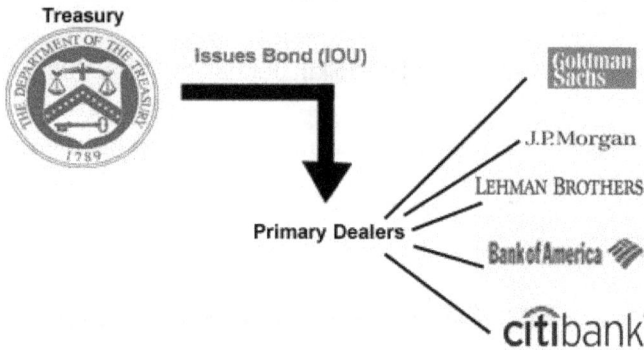

Step 2 The Fed will buy I Own You and Print Money...

Through open market operation, the Fed buys or sells bonds with the primary dealers. When it buys bond, it adds liquidity to the system. That means it prints money to expand the money supply. Conversely, if it sells bonds to the primary dealers, it drains liquidity from the system and money is withdrawn. So less money is circulated in the economy. The main difference between the Fed and primary dealers' bond purchase is that The Fed is creating money to buy it while others are buying it with money with value.

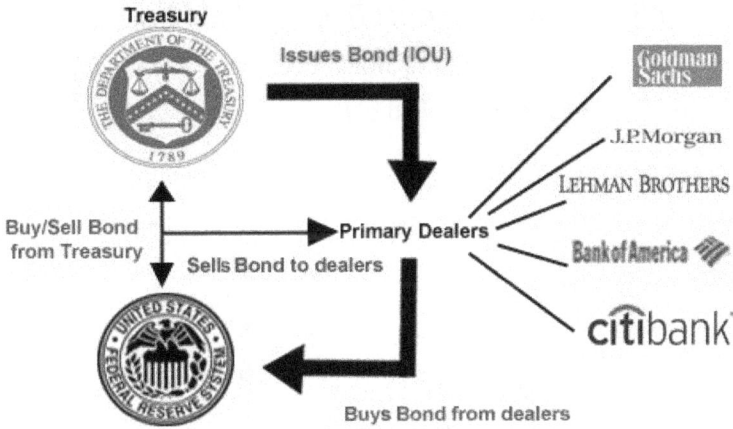

Step 3 Money created deposits into banks.....

The whole process can be simplified as the Fed buying bonds to expand the currency supply while the Treasury collects that money and pays for

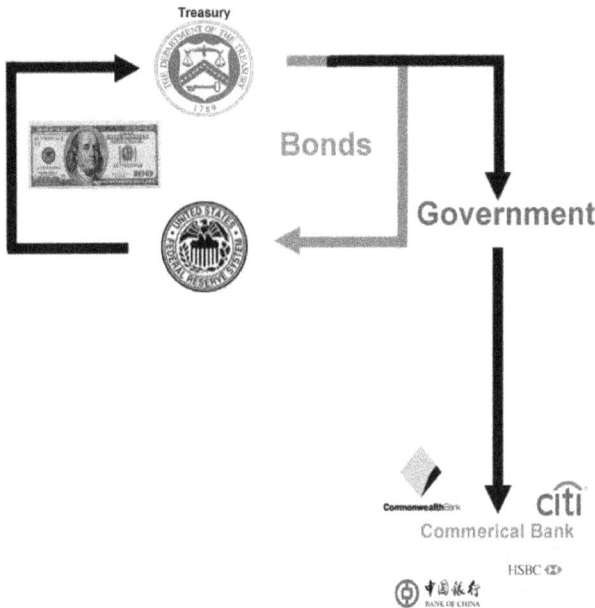

government bills like Medicare, social welfare, education, bailout of companies, buying MBS etc. The money paid to government employees will be deposited into commercial banks and then circulated in our economy.

Step 4 And Multiplied by Fractional Reserve Banking...

Then the commercial banks will use fractional reserve banking to multiply the currency supply, loan out money and collect interests.

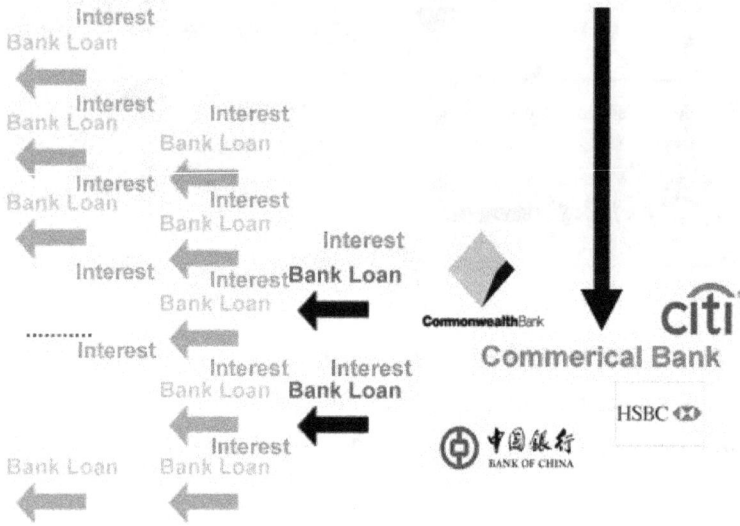

Step 5 Then we work hard and get taxed on it….

When this money is circulated in the economy, people work off that money supply so that we can pay taxes to the tax office. Then the tax office turn over the taxes collected to the Treasury Department so that it can pay the principal plus the interest on the bond that was purchased from the Fed out of nothing!

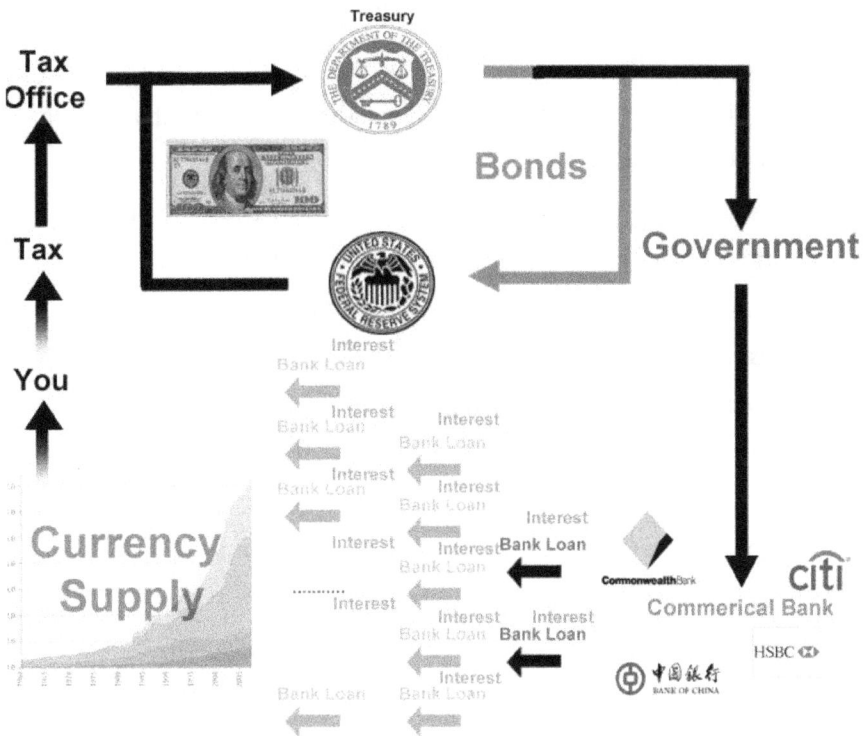

If you think about it, most people pay income tax. Every dollar in existence is a promise (Bond) to tax us until the day we die. The entire currency supply is owned back plus interest. Because there are interests due on loans and bonds, so there are always more debts in existence than money. We can never pay off our debts. This is the game we are playing.

Chapter 3

How Much is One Dollar?

My Grandad once asked me "How much is one dollar?"

"Um…A dollar is a dollar, right?" I honestly don't know the answer even though I have been using many dollars for years.

"No. when you say a dollar is a dollar, you are lying. By the time, you say that, a dollar does not worth a dollar anymore. Never be the person who blindly earns the dollar. Be the person who understands the dollar."

For years, I was puzzled about the message Grandad was trying to get across. A dollar clearly is one dollar, right? It even has one dollar stamped on it. What else do I need to understand about it? It was not until when I make my first million from my investment then I truly begin to see the real questions behind the wisdom of his words. What exactly is a dollar? Where does it come from? How do we define it? If you ask ten random people, I bet you will have different answers. The primary reason why world of finance is so complex today is because the definition of money becomes so ambiguous and subjective. The world has more money than the past, yet our prosperity seems to go backwards. Everyone wants to earn more money, yet very few understand it. It is ironic to spend the entire life earning something you do not really understand. Don't be one of them. I promise you, by the end of this chapter you will have a concrete understanding of what money really is.

What is Ten Dollars?

Some years ago, Mr. A.F. Davis mailed a ten dollar Federal Reserve Note to the Treasury Department. In his letter, he called for attention to the inscription on the bill which said the ten dollar note was redeemable for *lawful money,* and requested that lawful money to be sent to him. In reply, the Treasury just sent him back two $5 notes with the same inscription as the $10 note. He received the following response.

Dear Sir,

Receipt is hereby acknowledged of two $5 United State Notes, which we interpret from your letter are to be considered as lawful money. Are we to infer from this that Federal Reserve Note are not lawful money?

I am enclosing one of the $5 note which you sent to me. I note that it states on the face, "The United States of America will pay to the bearer on demand five dollar" I am hereby demanding five dollars.

On week later, Mr. Davis received a reply from Acting Treasurer, M.E. Slindee:

Dear Mr. Davis:

Receipt is acknowledged of your letter of December 23rd transmitting one $5 United State Notes with a demand for payment of five dollars. You are advised that the term "lawful money" has not been defined in federal legislation. ... The term "lawful money" no longer has such special significance. The $5 United States Note received with your letter of December 23rd is returned herewith.

The phase "*...will pay to the bearer on demand....*" and "*...is redeemable in lawful money.....*" were deleted from our banknotes altogether in 1964.

So can money be classified as lawful or unlawful? If so, are we all earning lawful money? What were those removed statements on the banknotes suppose to mean? Before we answer these questions, let's see what the Federal Reserve thinks money is.

Does the Federal Reserve Really Understand About Lawful Money?

On July 13th 2011, in a U.S. House Financial Services Committee Meeting, Congressman Ron Paul questioned the Fed's chairman on the concept of money. Here is the dialogue of the conversation.

Congressman Ron Paul

"The price of gold today is $1,580, the dollar in the last three years almost devalue 50%. When you wake up in the morning, do you care about the price of gold?"

Chairman of the Federal Reserve, Ben Bernanke

"I pay attention to the price of gold, but I think it reflects a lot of things. It reflects global uncertainties, the reasons why people own gold is to protect against what is called tail risk, that is really, really, bad outcomes. And to the extent of the last few years, this makes people more worried about the potential of a major crisis, then they have gold as a protection."

Congressman Ron Paul

"Do you think gold is money?"

silent…

Chairman of the Federal Reserve, Ben Bernanke

"No……It is a precious metal…"

Congressman Ron Paul

"Even if it has been money for 6,000 years, somebody reversed and eliminated that economic law?"

Chairman of the Federal Reserve, Ben Bernanke

"Well....It is an asset. I mean...it is the same if you ask if Treasury Bill is money. I don't think they are money either. I think they are financial assets."

Congressman Ron Paul

"Why do central banks hold it?"

silent...

Chairman of the Federal Reserve, Ben Bernanke

"It is a form of reserve."

Congressman Ron Paul

"Why don't they hold diamonds?"

Chairman of the Federal Reserve, Ben Bernanke

"Well, it is tradition."

Mystery of Money

My Grandad had a unique way of understanding and describing money. When I was a kid, Grandad used stories and diagrams to teach me his theory on money. In the following pages, I offer you the same basic foundation that Grandad had created for me. Though simple, these drawings help me earned my small fortune. If you are ready, say I am ready.

Concept Number 1 Before money

It may surprise you that money does not originally come from the government or the states. It was invented naturally by Free Market base on the needs of transactions. Before money existed, the society had functioned on the barter system. Suppose you are good at fishing, you can produce a surplus of fish to exchange for something produced by others. Everyone exchange something they need less for something they need more. These trades are mutually benefited. There was no such thing as money.

Concept Number 2 Why we need money?

But one problem arose, different people value things differently at different times. Say, if you want to buy eggs, you would have to find an egg seller, who at the same time also has the same desire of fish. If the egg seller does not like fish but salt, then you will have to rush off to find a salt dealer who wants fish and trade with him before doing business with an egg seller. So the first problem is *double consistence of want* for the exchange to happen.

The second problem is in *indivisibility*. If you want to sell your house for cars, yachts or other things, obviously you cannot chop your house into pieces and sell it piece by piece, otherwise it will lose all the value. So house is not divisible for barter. In this case, there will not be as many house produced apart from living.

You can imagine how inefficient barter system can be if it is to function in our modern society. There will be fewer business transactions take place. The total productivity of the society will be greatly diminished. Because of these limitations, it laid the foundation that drives us human to re-think.

The society needs something that everyone or the majority of the population wants. So instead of trading one product directly with another, people trade his surplus with a generally accepted *thing* first, and then use it to exchange for what he wants to buy. Going back to our case, it means Marco does not buy salt because he wants salt; he buys salt because he knows everyone need salt at some point. Salt can be used as a medium to barter things he wants to buy now or in the future. So salt became an indirect exchange. Also, now people can use salt for commerce. A company can express their loss and gain in the amount of salt so that they can understand how well they are doing. Our income and expenditure can be express in salt. That's means people can now save and invest. It is a great leap in our economy. This forms the foundation of money as *a unit of account*.

Concept Number 3 What constitutes money?

Salt seems to be good as money. But there is one problem. If salt get wet, it dissolves! So storing wealth in salt and watching it dissolves in bad weather might not be a very good idea. Durability becomes a problem. Money needs to be preserved for a long period of time.

Throughout history, human experimented different commodities to be used as money. Cows, shells, rice, fish, salt and copper were only a few on the list. Even cigars were used as money during WWII. But each of them has advantages and drawbacks. Fish was used as money at some stage but sizes and breed matters. Who would want a dying goldfish for transactions if everyone is expecting a healthy salmon? So fungibility is crucial. Each unit of money must be equivalent to another unit of money. That explains why diamond is not used as money.

Slowly, through trial and error, people discovered to use metals as money. Copper seems to fulfill all the characteristic of money, but there are two problems. It is too easy to find, and bloody heavy to carry around! But you can make copper smaller, right? Certainly we can. But copper are far too abundant relative to the goods we want to buy. If something is too abundant, it tends to be less valuable. This is the same reason why beautiful girls are of high value. They are hard to come by. Also portability is a problem. Who would like to hold a few kilos of copper bars around just to transact for a Mars chocolate bar, right? To solve that problem, people need to search for something relatively scarce to the things they want to buy. That thing needs to have high value per unit weight. Money needs to be valuable.

Now the framework of money becomes clearer. Throughout history, human discovered that money need to have the following characteristics:

1. A medium of exchange
2. A unit of account
3. Divisible
4. Durable
5. Fungible
6. Portable
7. Store of value

Concept Number 4 Money is expressed in weight

Throughout history in civilization, there are only two commodities that truly demonstrated their role as money – Gold and Silver. They have been used as money for more than 5,000 years. Gold and silver are ranked as precious metal because of scarcity. Scarcity and precious are what creates value. Each year, there is only a certain quantity of gold minted. So the quantity is quite predictable and stable. In fact, all the gold mined in history still exists today. Even for a small increment in gold supply every year, it is always scarce compared with other things. This is what makes gold suitable to act as the world total money supply.

The concept of gold and silver as money form the foundation of coinage. Each coin has a defined weight. That's why weight defines value. You may be surprised to know that currency of countries such as *dollar, pound, mark* etc are simply names for different weight for gold and silver. The unit *dollar* we use every day is actually originated as the name of one ounce of silver coin minted by Bohemian Count named Schlick in the sixteenth century. The currency *pound* sterling in Britain means exactly one pound of silver. So the exchange rate we are using today is actually based on the weight of gold and silver defined.

Concept Number 5 Money in our pockets toady are not money

Civilizations flourished once they substitute other commodities with gold and silver for commerce. It became like a magic formula to prosperity. As society evolved and become more complex, holding and storing physical gold and silver at home became insecure. This gave birth to the idea of paper currency. Instead of self storage and risk theft, people decided to deposit their metals in commercial banks. The banks issues government legal tender banknotes as a representation of their deposit. In other words, the banknotes were receipts of gold and silver. They are not money. Their values are base on trust of banks such that depositors can redeem their metals. In theory, the total money supply should be the sum of all the banknotes issued by banks. The total value of these banknotes should reflect the weight of all the gold ever minted. If the total amount of banknotes in circulation is more than the total weight of the metals deposited. This means the value of the metal is stolen. This is why the so-called money we are using today is not really money. Money should be a store of value.

How Much is One Dollar?

"So how much is one dollar, Grandad?"

"I am glad you asked." Grandad smiled. "Before I answer you, you need to know something. Once you know it, you can use this as a tool to understand money."

"What is this tool!" I cried excitedly.

"This tool is called the *Free Market*."

Grandad put down his coffee and began to draw something on a piece of paper. It was a diagram with two lines, one horizontal and one vertical, and some numbers on the bottom and an S on the top. "Let's take Coffee for example. What does it mean to have 10 million pounds of coffee for consumption? How do we show it on paper?"

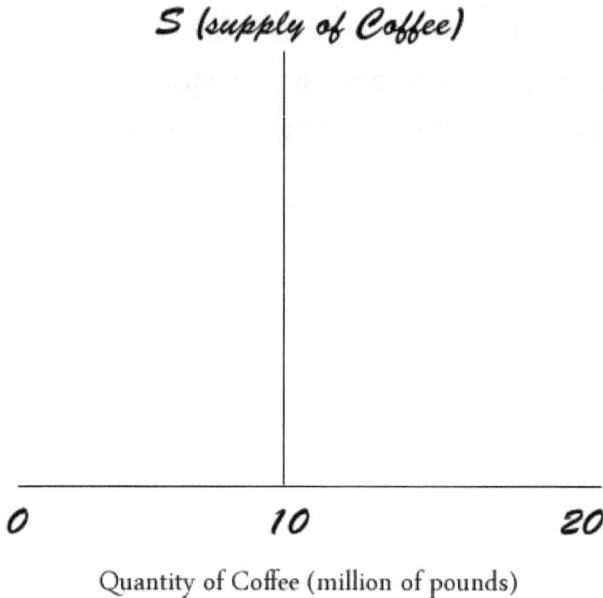

S (supply of Coffee)

Quantity of Coffee (million of pounds)

I scratched my head.

"The horizontal line is the quantity of coffee produced. I put a scale from 0 to 20 million pounds. So 10 million pounds set right in the middle. To have 10 million pounds of coffee for consumption, someone must be able to supply that quantity. The vertical line is the supply line with an S symbol. The supply line represents 10 million pounds of coffee can be supplied for consumption."

"If the supply of coffee becomes 5 million pounds, the supply curve shifts to the left. On the other hand, if the supply of coffee is 15 million pounds, the supply curve shifts to the right."

"Exactly." Grandad nodded. "Now what about the demand for coffee in the free market? In general, the law of nature tells us that the higher the price of something, the less demand we have for it. Our demand of coffee is probably not the same. Different people value things differently. I like coffee and you don't, so I am willing to pay a higher price for the same quality of coffee than you. Does it make any sense?"

"Yes. If I don't like coffee, even though you give me 20 million pounds of coffee, maybe I am just willing to pay $10 for it. But if you like coffee so much, maybe you are willing to pay $100 for a couple hundreds of pounds."

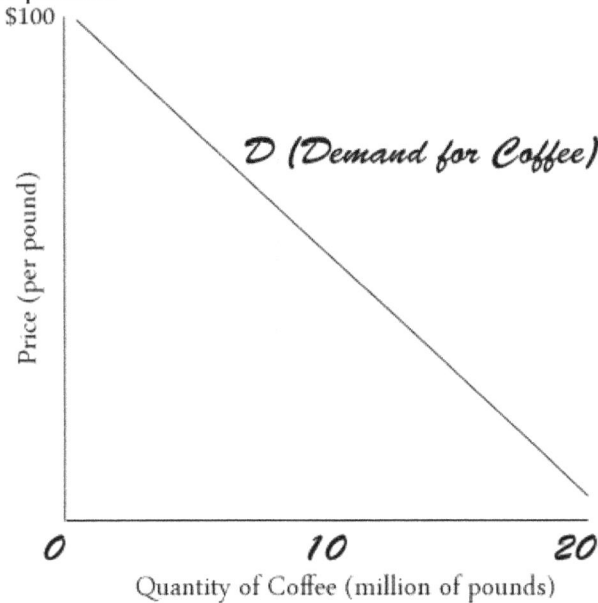

Quantity of Coffee (million of pounds)

"You got the point. This diagram is an ideal way of describing what you were saying just then. This is the demand curve. The curve does not have to be a falling straight line (negative slope). It can be a curve or even a zigzag shape. But the idea is still the same. The higher the price, the less will be purchased. That's why the curve is negative slope."

"Interesting! This curve describes a lot of things about

human actions. Do these graphs have any relationships?"

"Yes. They do. If you put two graphs together, it tells you a story. You see the black dot on the graph. It is the intersection point between the D and S curves. The price of 10 million pounds of coffee under a free market is $10 per pound. This is the price what the market would pay. It is the *fair market value*. The supermarket must set the price of their goods as close to the fair market value as possible to have most of the good sold to maximize profits."

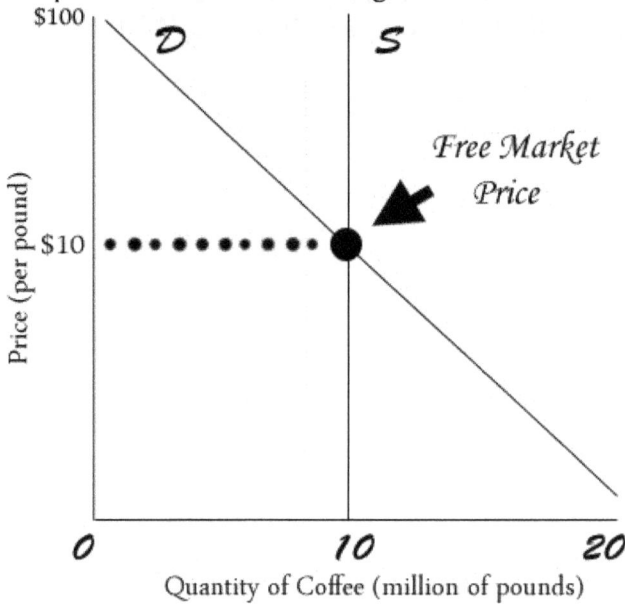

Quantity of Coffee (million of pounds)

"This is a very interesting concept. A company must not set their price too high, otherwise it has excess inventory on self. But it cannot set their price too low either, otherwise they will lose some profits. But Grandad, how does this fit into the dollar story?"

"Good question. If you think about it, everything in our society has a money-price of their own- except one remaining thing. That is Money."

"But can we price money with money? One-dollar is equal to one dollar right?"

"We can price money. Money has a good-price of its own. It is call purchasing power of money (PPM). It is to measure how valuable is your money. PPM is the inverse of the price of goods. In fact before money was invented people used to price one thing with another. Phases like the horse price of shoes, or the salt price of books were not uncommon. Price is simply the ratio of one quantity over another."

$$\text{Purchasing Power of Money (PPM)} = \frac{1}{\text{Price}}$$

"I see. Because there is more and more money created through the financial system, everything else appears to become more expensive. The *money* we hold will only continue to lose purchasing power."

"You are following." Grandad smiled and drew another diagram. "So if you replace the example of coffee with money, you will get this picture. S is the money supply. Horizontal axis is the quantity of money in circulation. Vertical axis is the purchasing power of money. If you increase the money supply by shifting it to the right, you will find that the dollar you are holding will have less purchasing power. Since we have an ever expanding money supply, that is why the value of one dollar is different everyday."

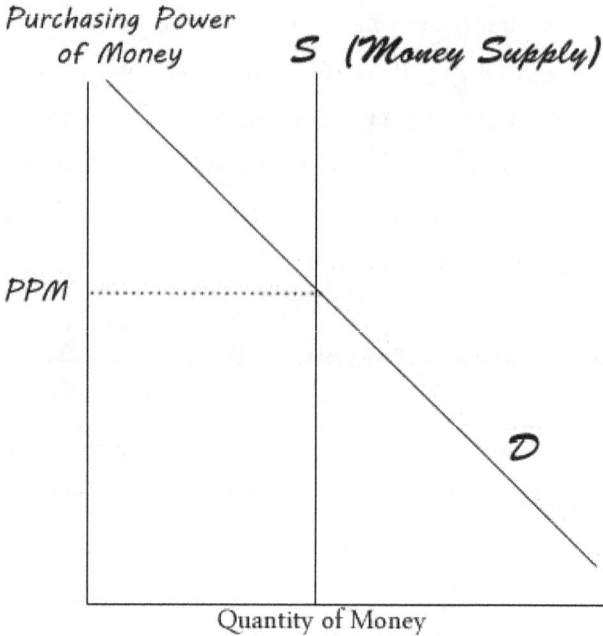

Lesson 4:

The more money is created, the less purchasing power (valuable) our money has.

Are We all Earning Money?

Understanding money is particularly important to defy corruption of Real money. I do believe we are not earning what we called money today. The nature of money had changed. Today, money can be created at will through the financial system. That's why it has a special name called *fiat currency.* Fiat means it is mandated by government. Currency is derived from the word current. If you study physics, you will know current must continue to flow otherwise it dies off. That's why currency must be invested and moves from one asset to another otherwise it loses value. So earning fiat currency means you are earning money designed to lose value.

Lesson 5:

We are earning fiat currency today. Fiat currency is not money. It is designed to lose value.

In pervious chapters, I have been using the word "money" very loosely. But now we understand the difference between currency and money. I will use the correct term throughout the rest of the book.

Take Away – The Origin of the Dollar.

U.S. Constitution states that *"Congress shall have the power to coin money and regulate the value thereof"*. It means that Congress was given the power to take gold and silver, which the country recognized as money, and mint them into coinage form for commerce. In Article I, Section 10 of the U.S. Constitution, it forbids anything other than gold and silver coin for debt settlement. Only gold and silver are lawful money. The dollar was first defined in the Mint Act of 1792 as 371.25 grains of fine silver.

Chapter 4

The Great Lies of Government

"When the government in pursuit of good intentions, tries to rearrange the economy, legislate morality, or help special interests, the cost come in inefficient, lack of innovation, and loss of freedom. Government should be a referee, not an active player."

-Milton Friedman

If NASA had evidenced the same level of understanding about physics as our government understanding of economics, the Apollo 11 mission would probably have had very different outcomes. Not only might the Apollo crew-members never reach the moon. The whole mission might spell a disaster recorded in history for generations. No one had summarized government interventions more elegantly than Milton Friedman. Under a free market society, government's role should be limited to enforcing contracts, legislate fairness, and making sure laws are not broken. These are the government's job and should be the government's only job. When the government gets fancy to interfere the market by making promises, whether or not in good intentions, it will always induce unintended outcomes.

This chapter is about government's great lies. It almost did not make into this book. However, I believed the information presented in this chapter is far too important to be cut out. It is the third pillar to grassroots the corruption of real money One of the philosophies we have today is that the government is there to take care of everybody. Whenever we face a social problem, government must interfere. Ironically solving one problem will give birth to another one. When the government tries to raise minimum wages where they seem fair and jobs go overseas. When the government set interest rate low to prevent a recession and a housing bubble is created accidentally.

In reality, these social problems exist for a reason. It is the free market signaling us for corrections. While free market solutions are bitter, people always want an easy way out. We all have self interests. It is human nature. That is why people seek help from the government. But the problems with government solutions are like putting fire on gasoline. It tends to make things worse in the long run. Now the problems become too big that it is already too much for this generation to shoulder.

Is There Such a Thing Call Free Lunch?

Do you believe in Free lunch? I don't. I believe everything comes with a price tag. Recently, I came across a video on Milton Friedman economic titled *Free Lunch Myth*. Even as an old clip, the theories presented are more applicable to explain modern economic thinking than any time in history.

There are two free lunch myths that people buy into even today. The first one is taxing big corporations. Politicians buy votes by reducing income tax while raising tax on the rich and large corporations. As fair as it might sounds, actually it is nothing more than a bookkeeping accounting trick. Let's think about what's business tax. Can businesses be taxed? Can the buildings pay taxes? No. If you boil down to the essence, only people can pay taxes. These taxes need to pay by somebody, either by the employees, the business owners, the customers or stockholders. In order words, even the companies are taxed, the cost will always be shifted indirectly to the third party. When a company writes a check to the tax office, someone else bear the dollar cost. The so-called tax to the employer is most likely paid by the employees if not the customers.

Lesson 6:

When government says we must not increase tax on individuals, we increase tax on business, what that means is that the cost is most likely passed on to the customers, stockholders or the employees. Instead of fighting for increasing taxes for corporation, we should vote for eliminating the tax on corporations once and for all.

Another free lunch myth is that people seems to think that the government bank account is unlimited. They think that currencies can be printed at no cost. It is as cheap to print a $100 banknote as it is for $10. But does that actually cost the society something for nothing? Not at all, printing currencies out of thin air is simply just another form of taxation. If the government prints more currencies, people will spend it to buy things. As more and more currencies are printed relative to the goods and services, prices will go up. In fact, everyone at the end of the day will pay tax through inflation.

Lesson 7:

When government prints more currencies relative to the goods and services in the economy, prices go up. This is called inflation. Inflation is just another form of taxation.

The Wrestle of Invisible Hands

"Ching, do you believe in invisible hands?" My Grandad and I were in his library. He was holding a book titled the *Wealth of Nations*.

"What are invisible hands?"

"Imagine for every actions you take, every decisions you made for yourself, is actually led by an invisible hand without your intention."

Government Forces   **Market Forces**
(Hand of the States)   **(Invisible Hand)**

"Really? Is that possible?" I asked curiously.

"An invisible hand is like a giant hand, people are like prawns in chess and the chessboard is our economy. In order for a butcher or a banker to make a profit, he has to produce something that someone want to buy so in the process to fulfill his self-interest, he ended up serving his customer. This is the free market."

"So an invisible hand leads people who originally serve private interest ended up also serving the public interest with no part of their intentions."

"Yes. Unfortunately, in the political market there is another invisible hand operating in the exact opposite direction. This is the hand of the state, which is originally designed to serve public interests but ended up serving special interests concentrated to a few people. It is an unseen wrestle, unknown by most of the people it affects. Yet, we all feel the effects of this epic battle in our daily lives. Whether it is on education, healthcare, social securities, poverty or wages, the wrestle between the market force and the government forces always continue. Most people think the hand of the State will always win. They have blind faith that the government can overwhelm the free market force. However, the truth is that the power of the market is much greater than the states. That's why the social problems we face today will only be worsen."

"After all these years, after so many elections campaigns were run, it is apparent to me that it doesn't matter who won as the president. Government continues to grow so long as we believe the way to solve our social problems is to turn them over to the government." Grandad continued.

Stop Lying please...We Knew it!

One morning I was accompanying Grandma to the wet market. Wet market is also called the fresh food market. The term wet market comes from the extensive use of water to clean the floor to keep fruits and vegetables fresh, and the fish alive. This is the place where you will see chicken got beheaded and frogs being skinned alive. So a wet market is simply a slaughtering house of livestock. Believe me, if you are a tourist, please take my words and skip the wet markets. Despite the poor hygiene conditions, I had a mission to go there, not to see chickens getting beheaded, but to gather information for Grandad to build a secret system.

"What do you have for me, Ching?" Grandad sat patiently in front of his computer as I passed him my notes gathered from the wet market.

"Wow. 6 percent!" Grandad exclaimed.

"What do you mean by 6 percent?" I ask curiously. All I saw were records of numbers from my notes reentered in Microsoft excel spreadsheet. It was an index with the name of things as columns and date as rows. Each cells shown the prices of things for a particular day. These things included chickens, beef and many other commodities. Seriously I have been doing this for Grandad for many months, but I had no clues of his intentions.

"Do you remember the price of one dollar?"

"Yes. I do. It is the good prices. It is the purchasing power of goods."

"Very good. The price you have been gathering for me is very important to understand the good price of the dollar. The reason we are doing this is because I don't believe our government is being very honest."

"Huh? You mean our government is lying?" I sound suspicious.

Grandad browsed the figure on the government website. "Here it is. 2 percent inflation rate on the website and a 6 percent in our spreadsheet. Ching, are you lying?"

"No! Definitely not. These are figures I checked in the wet market and other stores." I tried to defend myself.

"Then the wet market and other stores are lying." Grandad teased.

I remained speechless and confused. The figures were definitely right. Things have definitely gone up. But why was the inflation still remains at 2%?

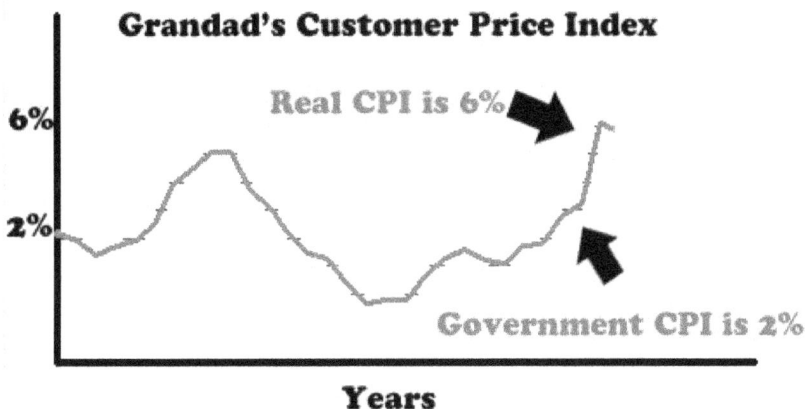

Grandad's Customer Price Index

"I know why. They forgot to update their website."

Grandad chuckled. He had shown me a document from his draw. It was a hand-made graph. "Wow Grandad! Did you draw all this by hand? How long have you been doing this? It was dated back even before I was born!"

"I have been tracking down the price of commodities since 1982 with base value of $100. This graph is called a customer price index (CPI). It is used to track down the effects of inflation but not the inflation itself. Inflation is the printing of currencies, rising prices are the result of inflation."

"What is the difference?"

"When the government creates currencies, this action is called inflation. But prices will not instantly rise when the government crunches the printing press. It takes time for these newly created currencies to flow into the economy. Once they got spent, then we will see the price rise. So Ching, do you know who get the most benefit out of this?"

"No."I scratched my head.

"The people who get the currency first and spend it."

"I see. It is because they spend it before the customer price rises."

"The fair way to measure CPI is by weighting a fixed basket of goods.

	Milk	**Bread**	**Beef**
One Year Ago	**$2.75**	**$2**	**$5**
Today	**$3.75**	**$2.5**	**$11**

Suppose you and grandma brought 5 gallons of milk, 5 loaf of bread, and 1 kg of beef per month, the cost of these goods would be a total of $28.75 per month calculated from last year. Now if you want the buy the same basket of goods, it costs you $42.25 per month this year. When you subtract the difference and then divide it by last year's amount and then convert it in percentage, you will get 47%. This is the increase in CPI for a gallon of milk, a loaf of bread and a kilo of beef."

"Wow, hey Grandad but how come we got 6 percent?"

"Good question. Do you realize the size of the basket of goods when you go out and gather data for me? I specifically ask you to gather price on food and energy as they are more sensitive to price inflation. They determine the core inflation. The more core samples you gather, the more reliable the data is. The ones we have in the spreadsheet is the closest one to the governments."

"But how come the government got a lower CPI?"

"Because these government indexes are creatively adjusted. There are three methods the government uses to manipulate the CPI. The first one is by substitution method. Let's say if the price of beef rises, people will switch to something relatively cheaper, say pork for example, now the CPI basket substitutes beef with pork. Does that means there is no price increase in beef? No. It is simply not included in the formula."

"So every time the price of something goes up, the government will substitute it and replace with something cheaper." I responded.

"Exactly. It's like in summer time when a person is sitting in his air-conditioned room enjoying his filet mignon. After the inflationary years, the same person in the same room can only afford to eat canned food and cool himself with fan. With the same amount of currencies spend on both cases, the CPI records there is no inflation under the current way of measurement. After all, he is cool and still eating."

"Wow! I wouldn't call that no difference. What about the second method?"

"The second method is by reducing the amount of things needed to be reported in CPI. If the CPI contains a basket of goods like computers, food and books etc. Removing food will significantly lower the overall reported value. In fact, U.S. President Nixon once tried to convince the public that the so-called core-inflation measure for CPI will strip out food and fuels."

"There is no point to measure inflation if you minus foods, drinks, fuels or energy…"

"To me, it is very strange. No wonder a financial commentator Barry Ritholtz says it is like measuring inflation ex-inflation. Just like ordering ice-lemon tea ex-lemon."

"Haha. What about the final one?"

"The final method is the most dramatic way the government uses to measure CPI. It is called hedonics adjustment. In Greeks terms, it means *"for the pleasure of"*. It is a form of adjustment to measure the improvement of products which leads to an improvement in quality of life. For example, if a new car costed $4,000 in 1967 and by 1999, the car costed $20,000, there was a five fold increase in price, right?"

"Agree. But how does hedonics adjustment distorts the CPI in this case?"

"The answer lies in quality improvement. There are many improvements in automobile like weight, functionality and design etc. So instead of reporting $20,000, the government adjusted the reported figure down to say $10,000. Now the increase halves."

"Wow. That's a lot. But how does the government quantify this decrease?"

"The government can do whatever they want with statistic which basically renders the CPI worthless. Improvement in quality is abstract and subjective. If the price of something goes up 50%, but the government thinks it is 60% better, so the overall price goes down 10%. So they report there is no or little inflation. That's why another word for CPI is CP Lie."

"Grandad I don't understand one thing. Why does the government have to lie?"

Lesson 8:
CPI is not a tool to measure inflation, it is a tool to track down the result of inflation.

Why The Government Has to Lie?

"Ching, do you remembered the last chief executive election we watched last month?"

"Yes I remembered. One political party promised to make more affordable education and housing by increasing loan limit and lowering the requirement. Another one promised to solve poverty by lowering tax, increasing social benefits and healthcare. In the end, you say you will support neither. But why?"

"Correct. I support neither because what they are saying make very little sense to me."

"But isn't that what everyone wants?"

"No. That's what everyone likes to hear only."

"Huh. I still don't understand."

"A lot of people find it difficult to understand this concept. In order to provide public services, the government needs revenues. The revenues come from the taxpayers. The problem is that people want the services on the expense of others. No one wants their tax to increase. If a politician says to the public he wants to raise taxes, it is political suicide."

"But if he can't raise taxes, where can he get the revenues?"

"Our government has a silent partner called inflation. It is a way to steal wealth away from the public without them even noticing it. Ironically, people accept it, they love it, they even vote for it."

"But the politicians say they even want to combat inflation in their debate." I argued.

"And the CPI is showing they are doing a good job." Grandad smiled.

"So that's the reason why CPI is kept low." I begin to see the entire picture.

"More to that, conventional textbooks you will study in the future defines inflation as a natural phenomenon. The real reason behind is because the government does not want you to know inflation is caused by them. They want you to buy into the idea that, inflation is caused by various factors like real economic growth, labor union demand for higher wages, greedy businessman pushing prices up, natural disasters or all of the above. Just not the government."

"That's very sneaky and carefully planned out." I shook my head in agreement.

"Indeed. To provide public services, the government either has to raise revenue from taxes or through inflation. It is a choice between taxing the current generation to support the public need or taxing the future generation for current needs."

"To survive in politics, the latter one is always a better option."

"But that is so unfair! Why doesn't anyone protest against it."

"Haha. Good question. They don't know or care about it like you are doing now. Ignorance is part of the human nature. Most likely people will not pay attentions to things which does not directly affects them. If the government raise tax, the policy directly affects the public. But if you create currencies, the future generation won't feel it until it is too late. By the time people feel it, someone else might be in the government office."

Government's Report Card Always Get 'A's

"Ching. Have you ever cheated on your exams?" Grandad pretended to ask seriously.

"Huh? Grandad, why do you suddenly bring up such a topic?"

"At school, every student has a report card to show their academic performance. In real life, everyone has a report card called financial statement. At national level, do you know our government has a report card as well?"

"Really? What is it called? What grades does government gets?" I felt excited.

"It is called Gross Domestic Product (GDP). Put it in this way, if you do well in school, you get 'A's, right? Well, if the economy grows by 2% or more, that means government is doing a good job. At least that is what most people think."

"So in order for the government to do a good job, that means the economy must grow."

"This is exactly what the government thinks. But in reality, this philosophy is a receipt of disaster."

"Huh? Do you mean economic growth is no good?"

"No..." Grandad laughed. "I don't mean that. What I am saying is that the philosophy of economic must growth is flawed. If the economy does not grow, that means it shrinks. People will loss their jobs; company fails, stock market crashes and causes a spiral of other undesirable consequences."

"So people in charge must not allow that to happen! Our economic must grow indeed."

"In reality, nothing grows forever. After expansions come contractions and after contractions come expansions. Our economy follows the law of nature, like the sunrise and sunset. This is called economic cycle."

"Nothing grows forever….."

"You are right. Most people know this, but few really understand this. Our government definitely does not understand it. If they do understand, then they will not continue to expand the currency supply at that kind of pace to prevent contractions. Some politicians in office do this in the name of helping people. Some do it for self-interest to be re-elected. Some do it because of the tradition. Whether it is good intention or not. This philosophy is very expensive."

"How is GDP formulated?"

"GDP has five components. The sum of these five components is how the government measures the economic growth." Grandad explained it on his whiteboard.

GDP components

1. Consumption
2. Investment
3. Government Spending
4. Import
5. Export

"When you are spending currencies to buy things, you are consuming. Consumption is positive for economic growth."

"It makes sense as the more people consume, they spend and stimulate the economy to move forward. GDP is a good indicator of economic growth." I added.

"Ching. Do you remember the tsunami of Indonesia?"

"Yes. It was terrible. The government spends a lot of currencies to rebuild. Survivors were fighting for necessities like crazy."

"It was a tragic event indeed. Since the government spent a lot to rebuild, if you follow the GDP logic, shouldn't the government be getting A+ in their report card?"

"Umm... Well in this case..."

"Let's take one step further. If GDP is such a good way to measure economic growth, then why don't we stimulate more disasters by first evacuate people in a city, then send out a group of 747 bombers to reduce the city into rubble and then promise the citizens in the city that we are going to replace their home with bigger and better houses. Do you think more economic growth can be generated that way? "

"Humm..." I was taking the time to digest the lesson.

"The reason why GDP doesn't make too much sense in this case is because it doesn't take economic loss into account. You see. Natural disaster destroys human capital, buildings and infrastructures. This means it causes the economy to go backward not forward. Economy grows by production, investment and saving. Productivity drives consumption to grow the economy. Sadly we are educated the other way around."

"It makes much more sense now. It seems the definition of GDP is flawed because it doesn't capture everything."

"Apart from the misleading way to measure GDP, hedonic experts are good at fabricating its statistics to measure GDP, so instead of getting a C for government's report card, they cheated for an A."

"Really? But how do they cheat this time?"

"For example, Company A manufactures a new computer which costs the same price as last year but with 10 times more processing power. Hedonic experts will assume that if the computer is 10 times faster, then people who use them will be 10 times more productive as well, is it true?"

"No. It depends on a lot of things. It depends on the person who is using it. It depends on how many hours it is operated productively etc."

"Yes. You get the point. If a million worth of computers is purchased, but equipped with 10 times more powerful microprocessors, the government should not report a sales of 10 millions when it calculates the GDP."

"This is not a right way to cheat to get an A." I smiled.

"The reason I tell you all these are to make you aware of government statistics. One of the main lessons in monetary education is to learn how to read government statistics with a very suspicious eye. Many people trust government statistic blindly, as a result, make the wrong financial decisions and never understand what really happened. To me, these statistics are the greatest lies in the history of the world."

Lesson 9:

GDP is not a good indicator to measure economic growth. Economic grows by production, saving and investment not consumption.

Can We Consume Our Way to Prosperity?

"*Growth* is a very important word. You can't read a single statement by a political leader without hearing the word growth dozen of times. Governments want to grow jobs. They want to grow the economy. Our GDP shows that consumption is the key to growth. In Australia, consumption accounts for 70% to 78% of GDP." Grandad explained.

Consumption Expenditure as a percentage of GDP in Australia

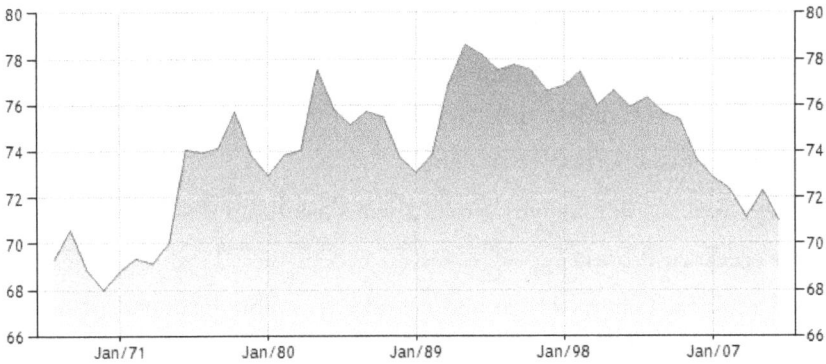

Source: World Bank Indicator- Australia –National Account

"But if our economy contracts and expands like you said, then when contraction comes, people have no currencies to consume. How did the government still managed to maintain growth of GDP at 2% years after years? "

"Theoretically if the economy contracts, people will have less currency to consume. But the government can still encourage people to spend more than they can afford."

"Do you mean by giving them currency?"

"No. They can only do that through tax return."

"Then how can the government help them?"

"By encouraging people to incur in debt, to spend now pay later. This way the government does not need to take a dime out from tax revenue, people have currencies to consume and government can get a good report card at the end of the financial year. So everyone is happy."

"How does debt works?"

"You see, when you borrow currencies from a bank, and pay interest on the loan, you incur debt. For example, if people want to buy furniture or TV but lack the cash, they use credit cards to finance their purchase. By using credit cards, and with their signature signed on the receipt, new currencies sprang into existence. These new currencies are not created because of productivity from you or me or anyone else on the planet. They are created out of one's signature and spent as if they are really money. Debt is a derivative of money. It is not money itself. The interest payable on debt is a derivative of debt."

"I always feel suspicious why banks always ask mom if she wants to raise her credit card limit."

"Yes. Credit card charges high interest rate. It is a big business itself. The reason why credit card lenders are so eager to loan out credits is because they can repackage your credit card debt and sell it on Wall Street. In 2010, Australia credit card debts alone accumulate up to $50 billion."

"$50 billion! Are there any examples how debt is used?"

"Of course. Credit card debt is one form of debt only, there are other debts like mortgages for housing, student loans for university degrees, business loans and the list can go on and on."

"So debts help people or business to finance things they cannot afford today, but the downside is that they have to pay more in the future because of the interest components."

"Exactly. If one person incurred in debts, someone must be credited. Debts and credits are both side of the same coin. In fact, if you remember how banks create currency, you will realize that debts, credits and loans are all interchangeable depending on the context."

"Interesting. But are all debt bad?"

"Depending on how people use it. If people are using debt to finance their luxury lifestyle and never have the intention to pay it back. This is bad debt. If you are using debt to help you to finance your university degree, and assume you can enhance your future income, then it is a good debt."

"How does the government encourages people to borrow more currency?"

"The government does that by reducing the interest rate. If you buy a house and you borrow money from the bank, the interest rate determines how much you pay back the bank on your mortgage."

"A higher interest rate means we pay more interest, and a lower interest rate means we pay a lower interest. Then of course we want a lower interest rate."

"This is exactly what the government wants too. They do this by keeping the interest rate artificially low. Interest rate is the demand and supply of money. By keeping the interest rate low and by lowering the requirement to borrow currency, people can get their hands on cheap credit easily. This boosts consumption and thus the government's report card."

"It seems that debt is the solution to many problems."

"It is a temporary solution in the short term. It seems as if the economy reaches a new era of unprecedented economic growth. However, debt is a time bomb for the economy in the long run."

"A time bomb?"

"The cheap credit borrowed and spent continues to dilute the currency supply. This flow of logic can be interpreted as stealing wealth from the future and spend it today. Eventually, debt borrowed need to be repaid."

"Who is going to pay for it?"

"Your generation."

"Huh? But I didn't incur these debts."

"I know. Your generation will pay it back either trough taxation, inflation or austerity measures (i.e. cutting social benefits). Once upon a time, for the economy to grow, productivity is important. You work hard and save money then invest the rest to become wealthy. Productivity drives prosperity. Today, this nature of the economy is distorted by debt. The birth of debt allows people to borrow the value of the currency from the future and buy what was once impossible to attain."

"But can our generation continue to borrow wealth from future indefinitely?"

"It is an economic fairy tale that government thinks people can consume their way to prosperity by using debts indefinitely. Some even think that the current debts fuelled economy is a new era. They religiously rely on the GDP. The sad part is that people are too ignorance to investigate the government data like what we did. If you read a newspaper, you will find out all sorts of social problems surfacing in employment, education, healthcare, employment, social security or poverty. Different sectors in the society are asking for more capitals from the government. The more the government gets involved, the worse things will become in the future. That's why government has to lie about statistic. This problem perpetuates."

"Is there a limit to how much we can borrow from the future?"

Is There a Limit to How Much we Borrow from the Future?

"Yes. It is called the debt to GDP ratio. But again this is a lying figure. It shows the optimistic way to understand what is happening. A healthy economic growth requires a GDP growth of 2% or more. If we have two consecutive negative GDP growth, it is called a recession. It means a F in the government report card. So the government encourage people to use debt to help them get an A. Debt to GDP ratio tells you how healthy is our economy."

"How does that work?"

"Imagine our economy as a patient, government as armature doctors, and debt as drugs. When the patient gets sick, instead of allowing self regeneration, the doctor recommends the use of drugs. Patients instantly feel better and think this doctor is an expert. But the problem is that the body never really recovers. Very soon he got sick again after the effects of drugs wear off. So what the doctor does is that this time he gives the patient a stronger drug. Each time the patient uses drug, the more he depends on it. This will reach a point where he overdoses and kills himself, not because of sickness but because of the drugs."

"I see. So by allowing the government to finance our problems through debt, the more we become dependent on the government. This will reach a point where government can no longer help us…"

"Exactly. Your body has a limit on how much drug you can take. Our economy has a limit on how much debt it can sustain."

Lesson 10:

Under a free market society, productivity drives economic growth. In our current economy, there is a misconception that consumption is the key driver instead. The truth is that production drives consumption. The reason our current economy can continue to grow is because our government finances it through debts. As the debt level grew faster than GDP, debtors become winners and savers become loser. Power shifted from industrial sectors to banking sectors. This is part of the reasons why banks have more influence on the economy than industries once had. Massively increasing debts can slow down the economic crash and portrait an illusion of recovery. But in the long run, debts need to be pay down. The prosperity we are enjoying now is at the expense of future generations.

Chapter 5
Robin Hood of the 21st Century

"The evil that is in the world almost always comes of ignorance, and good intentions may do as much harm as malevolence if they lack understanding."

-Albert Camus

"You know something', Robin. I was just wondering', are we good guys or bad guys? You know, I mean, uh? Our robbing' the rich to feed the poor." Little john asked.

"Rob? Tsk tsk tsk. That's a naughty word. We never rob. We just sort of borrow a bit from those who can afford it."

I loved Robin Hood cartoons when I was little. He was a hero, a famous outlaw. He became known for *"robbing the rich and giving it to the poor"*. I don't know why old cartoons always portrayed the rich as bad and greedy guys. Do you know why? Please email me if you do. Even now when I am writing this book, it still remains a mystery.

Although Robin Hood and his Merry Men might be long gone, his ideas and philosophy lives on. Today our government is doing exactly what Robin Hood was doing. Instead of "rob", they "tax", it is still borrowing a bit from those who can afford it. Government is playing the role of Robin Hood of the 21st century.

Midas Touch or Murphy's Touch?

In Greek mythology, King Midas had an ability to turn everything he touched into gold. Murphy's Touch does quite the opposite. Everything Murphy touches turn into shit. The Murphy's touch is the ideal metaphor to describe the failure of government interventions. This chapter discusses five social problems our government actively involves in. By the end of this chapter, you will understand why i consistently oppose to government intervening our social problems.

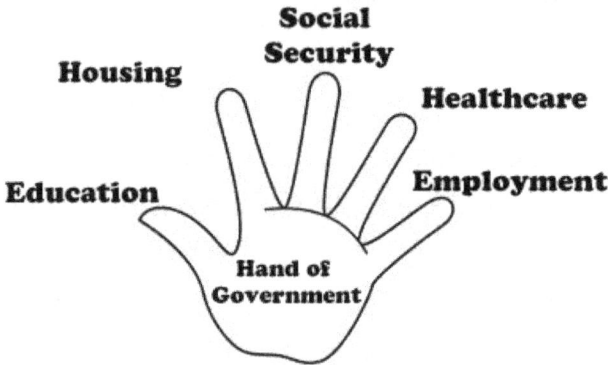

The Thumb : Education

Have you ever heard a politician say "Okay, that's enough spending on education" or " Let's cut spending on education"? It is taken for granted that spending on education is always a good thing. As a result, we do not have any limits as to how much money is being put into education. Please don't misunderstand my intentions as I favor education especially lifelong learning. Like my Grandad said. "Never too old to Learn". But my question is if our spending on education is worth the value?

Is University a Waste of Time and Money?

University fees are skyrocketing but have the quality skyrockets along? I am not referring to the quality of university life like fancy gyms, cutting edge student centers, or Macintosh PC installed on every bench of the main library. What I am talking about is the value of the degree, its costs and benefits. Most people would have guessed a doctor graduated would be way better off than a plumber. In reality, this does not always hold true. Today, going to universities can be worse than if you haven't enrolled. But how does that make any sense?

First, think of a university degree as an investment; it may or may not guarantee you to get back in the field you study. Next time when you go to a grocery, ask the cashier what her major was. She would probably tell you it was accounting or business. So one might just wasted three years of precious time with borrowed money or cheap finance. By the time of graduation, they only found themselves loaded up with debts, miserably struggling to seek for a job in their own field.

Second, when too many people graduate with a university degree, a degree becomes less valuable. In the past, I admit that a degree does make a difference in the workforce. It was a valuable asset for a job application. These days, students in Asia, found themselves the need for a master degree or even a PHD to be competitive. The result is that it dilutes the value of everyone's degree. It makes the employer feel a degree is less valuable. This makes the job market becomes tougher and tougher. Do you feel the same right now?

So Why University Costs so Much Today?

Have you realized that the demand for university degree is a very interesting subject. Each year, there seem to be bottomless demand of it. No matter how expensive it becomes, students and parents are willing to pay any price for it.

But how come more and more people seems to be able to get into university nowadays? Are we all wealthier? No. The main reason is because government gets involved in education business. They subsidy it. This can be originated back from U.S. president Lyndon Johnson signed the Higher Education Act of 1965 as part of his "*Great Society*" plan. The idea behind the act was to provide financial assistance to student for university education. The intention was noble as it provided students, who would be unaffordable otherwise, an opportunity to go to university by borrowing from the government. Later on, many other countries followed and legislated similar acts.

As the population grew, more and more students decided to go to university. Our tradition beliefs on education combine with employers' expectations drive even higher demand for university education. The result is that universities get more students, and thus more capital. To meet the student's demand, government must continue to increase the amount of subsidies. But the higher the subsidies, the higher the cost of going to universities, and this cycle perpetuates. Today a typical university graduate will be sitting on a $24,000 student loans at least. That's why government's intentions of making university degree affordable had achieved the exact opposite effect in the long run.

I remembered when my dad went to university, he graduated without any government or parent's financial support. He funded his university education all by himself through part-time tutoring. Is that possible for us today?

Who Gets the Benefits from All of These?

Do the students get more benefit out of student loans? I doubt it. If it is not the students, who get the benefits? I think it is the construction companies. Every time I pass by campus, I see constructions of new-cutting edge campus buildings, shiny gyms, and state of the art lecture theatres. Buildings are demolished and rebuilt. This is how our taxes are used. Also, the lending agencies are getting direct benefits out of this. As universities fees skyrocket, the more students will have to borrow. I once heard a young lady on a radio show, graduated with a sociology degree, sat on $200,000 in debt. It is hard to believe why the government would allow her to borrow that much in the first place. How can she repay all these loans? Does her degree worth that much? It makes me feel university education nowadays has become very commercial.

University Trap - Learning to be Broke

Most of us go to universities so that we can get educated, get a good paying job, not to live in a mansion, but to be independent and improve our standard of living. But today, the trend is that most people finishing their degree will move back to live with their parent. Some remain unemployed, but sitting in massive debt. Those who are employed maybe spending the whole life trying to pay back the principal of the loan. Even the payment depends on income tax bracket, the amount payable is inflation adjusted. That means the higher the inflation rate, the loan amount will be adjusted higher. While it seems fair to maintain the value of the borrowed money from the tax payers, it creates a trap for graduates to be a slave of debt. If you look beneath the surface, is it like a scheme to enslave graduates in debts in the name of education?

Why Does High School Education Becomes So Expensive too?

If you are a parent of kids, you will probably realize how costly it is to provide education to your kids all the way through K-12. A survey done by Australian Scholarships Group projects shows that the cost of K-12 schooling for children from 2013 will be around $47,290 for public schools and $535,842 for private schools! This is excluding all the textbook fees and other extracurricular activities.

One of the reasons why high school education becomes so unaffordable is because government tries to make it affordable. Does it make any sense to you? The government gets involved by subsidizing or giving allowance. It is true that these benefits will give a hand to those who cannot afford high school education in the short term. The price is that it increases the demand for schooling and causes the tuition fees to goes up. The more government subsidies, the more expensive education will become. That's why you see the cost of public school is going through the roof.

But what about private schoolings? Isn't it independent? The fact is that private schoolings are most likely more expensive than public schoolings. When demand of public school goes up, the demand for private school will only go higher. It is because parents are built in with the perception that private schools provide better quality education. A good education to their kids is always the first priority of most parents. Sending kids to private school is also a class distinction. So you see, there are a lot of built in factors like that. In reality, if a family financial situation allows, most parents will send their kids to private schools.

How to Bring Education Cost Back to Normal?

If you are looking for high quality education with low price, only the free market can provide that. This is done through competitions. Although it will be a huge milestone for the government to bring the education cost down to normal, but it can be done. The problem lies in the demand for education.

First the government should slowly cut all the allowances to aid public schoolings. The best time to cut will be when a student had all the essential skills they need to work in the society.(e.g. The first three years of high school). That way we can bring the demand down. Is this moral? Absolutely not, but our parents or grandparent did not receive government subsidies on education either. That was how the value of education was maintained. In reality, not everyone is college material, those who cannot afford can pursuit other interests in life and still end up being successful.

As the size of government school shrinks, demand of classes will shrink. Then the government can reduce their burden of allowance. Public tuitions fees will go down together with private tuition fees. More private schools will emerge through competitions. That is how the free market helps to improve the education quality and drive price down.

This receipt suggested in this book should be used as a transition strategy. It is not designed to be an overnight success. By getting government less involvement and appropriately reduce the demand of education, I believe education will be once again of high quality and low cost.

Index Finger: Housing

If you wonder why housing becomes so unaffordable today, once again you need to ask the government why get involved in it. While many who board the real estate train thought they would be safe because housing will always appreciate. It is a sure thing. I have a different point of view.

Why Housing Becomes So Unaffordable?

Housings in Sydney and Hong Kong now rank as two of the most unaffordable place in the world. The housing price in Hong Kong gone up 8.5 times in 33 years while Sydney home price gone up more than 6 times over the same period. While 6 times might not sound a lot to most people in such a long period, but if you consider a medium price home of $600,000 today compare to $100,000 33 years ago, it does means a lot to a lot of people. But our wages had an increase over the years right? If the wages increase cannot keep pace with the rising home price. That means housing is becoming more unaffordable even with a salary increase.

But how did the price get there in the first place? While some people say it is because of high demand from immigrants, some say it is because of inflation, and some say it depends on the locations. I agree with all of them because they can all be right base on subjectivity. But the root cause of are not those reasons. The main reason why housing keep climbing is government intervention and debt.

Remember our government does not like a bad report card. Every time we had a recession, unemployment strikes, and our government will step in as the savior. One of the sectors our government will save at all cost is the housing sector. Housing is like the backbone of the society. In fact, in some countries' balance sheet, household mortgage debt accounts for 70% of a country's liabilities. If household mortgage debt is allowed to collapse, it will turn a recession into a depression which takes years to recover. So what the government does is that it cuts the interest rate to a low level. This makes it easier for people to borrow more cheap credit from the banks. Borrowers will pay less monthly mortgage repayment under low interest rate.

In Australia, the government launched a series of policies called First Home Buyer Granted (FHBG). What this does is that it exempts stamp duty for young people who buy their first home, and grant them a certain amount of currency to start off. So FHBG with artificially low interest rate does their job by making it easier for people to board the train. But it creates a long term concern. Has this really make housing more affordable? What happens if the government intervention no longer works? What happen if the home price are too high that interest repayment under low interest rate are still difficult to repay.

If I Board the Real Estate Train....

Those who have yet to board the real estate train admire those who already have homeownership. For those who have real estate often pay more than half of their income on mortgage repayments. So many home owners have to lower their standard of living, spending their lives working for the boss and the banks. Does this sound familiar to you?

What if I own multiple properties? Government encourages people to buy properties because housing is the backbone of the economy. If you are not buying them with cash but debt, it means that the more properties you hold, the higher the leverage you have. One way people do that is by borrowing equity from one property and using it as a collateral to buy another one and so forth. But there is a plus and minus to everything. Leverage is a double sword. It can help a person to accumulate great wealth as long as the property price continues to rise. It is a very different story if property prices head south. For example, if a property price falls from $500,000 to $300,000. Assume you are taking out a 20% mortgage when buying this house, the $200,000 difference in price means you have to pay back to the bank instantly otherwise the bank has the right to withdraw your collateral. When that happens, years of saving is wiped out. That's why using leverage to buy more properties can be devastating, it is a double edge sword. Both the timing of entering and exiting the market are equally important.

Why People Think Real Estate Will Go Up

Statistics shows that Real Estate will always go up. Media uses propaganda to sell this idea. Government uses tax law to favor it. People buy into the idea that holding a few pieces of real estates can lead to great wealth. We know that past generations did this, and people buy into the belief it will work the same. While this strategy did work well in the past, it might do the exact opposite in this decade.

In the country I am living in at the moment, we have a government intervention called negative gearing. That means when a person buys a piece of property for investment, and if the property rental income is less than the interest payment of the property, then normally this means the person invests into that property for a loss. However, the government does not want that to happen as it discourages people to invest in real estate and weakens the housing market. So they promise to allow people to offset the investment loss against their income. In other words, interest payment on a mortgage is fully tax deductible. This policy maybe good but no investor would bother to ask why they would buy an asset that is so overvalued and offered a negative cash flow in real term.

But real estate will always go up, right? But will it? Does it make any sense for an asset to become so overvalued and offer negative returns, yet continue to appreciate? It is just going to collapse. But the people who bought real estate, and those still buying real estate, are making the same mistake as people who bought real estate at the peak during Asian Financial Crisis in 1997. They are not basing their judgment on the fundamental value of an asset. They are basing it on the belief that there is always going to be a fool accepting more losses because real estate will always go up.

If the government is not involved in real estate and was to let the free market seek for the fair market value, then housing could be more affordable. Government solution is a high price but low mortgage payment which makes real estate unaffordable. Free market solution is low prices. Artificially low interest rate, FHBG and negative gearing were intended to help investors and homeownership for the middle classes. However, it seems that these good intentions are doing as much harm as they were supposed to prevent.

Middle Finger: Social Security

Before explaining social security, I want to share with you an investment trick called Ponzi Scheme. Say, I have a good deal for you. Give me $1,000, I will return you 10% per month. If you do not withdraw your principal, you can continue to receive $100 every month. Where else can you find a deal like that? The rule is that you can withdraw your money anytime, but you will risk the loss of your 10%. Then one week later, I tell ten more people the same thing. When your month is up, you will receive the fruit of your investment. So what I am doing is merely robbing Peter to pay Paul. As more and more people buy into this investment trick, you would probably figure out what will happen at last. There won't be enough late comers to pay off the earlier ones. What then happens is, I will then default and the scheme collapses. This was exactly what happened to Charles Ponzi in 1920. He spent a lifetime in jail.

Origin of Social Security - The New Deal

Approximately 83 years ago, the world had an infamous economic crisis, it was called "*The Great Depression of 1930*". It was a world record. The effect was so devastating that it almost crumpled Wall Street. In U.S., almost 50% of the human work power was left unused. Banks failed. There was no deposit insurance back then. So when banks went down, people's life savings vaporized along with it. It was a scary thought. There was no social security. Everyone was on their own. My Grandad lived through the

1930 period as a kid.

To combat *The Great Depression*, President Roosevelt designed a social program to massively rearrange the economy and put people back to work. It was the biggest scale of government intervention back then. This program was called – *The New Deal*. If you have relatives who lived through 1930-1940, they would probably have stories to tell. In fact, many social programs like *Centrelink* in Australia, or *Social Welfare Department* in Hong Kong are byproducts of *The New Deal*.

One of *The New Deal* Social programs was called "*Make Work*", the goal of this program was to solve the unemployment problem by returning the unemployed back to the workforce. President Roosevelt signed a bill of $3.3 billions to create approximately 34,599 jobs. Most of these government financed jobs are building of hospitals, road, airports, national parks and schools. But spending such a vast amount of money to create these type of jobs had not helped the economy much. The economy had a temporary rebound but ended up worse than before the *New Deal* was launched. These jobs were merely used to assist people in distress and restore hope and confident in public temporarily. *National Recovery Administration* was founded to launch a series of schemes like minimum wages and enforce employer to make production and employment. By 1935, the government passed the *Social Security Act*. It was created to aid unemployment, welfare pensions, handicapped and needy children. This was the first time in history government took responsibility for people in need.

New Deal was strictly designed to be a temporary program. Remember the money spent on funding this program comes from the taxpayer or inflation. There are economic costs to it. It is taking resources from the productive to the unproductive. It is borrowing value of the currency in the future and help the economy through *The Great Depression*. During the *New Deal*, government expands tremendously. People become more and more dependent on the government. Initially, it begins with food stamps, over the years, many additional programs like Medicare, Medicaid, housing subsidies, student loans, pensions, public assistance were added. Through generations of adaptation to social security, people were built in the perception that this is the way how government should work. It is the role of government to be the Robin Hood. Well it is not.

Today, many people still think that *The New Deal* was the solution to *The Great Depression*. They believe that big government was the cure. They are wrong. Despite how hard President Roosevelt tried to prop up the economy, the Depression resurfaced in 1937. Production and profits resumed their declines. Unemployment was as high as it was in 1932. The worst thing of all, all the money spent on welfare rose from $9 million to $479 million by 1940. All this spending caused a lot of inflation in the money supply. Above all, the Federal Reserve became more powerful as government became more dependent on it to create inflation.

Lesson 11:

New Deal had fuelled the many social problems we are facing today. Big government is not a solution to them. It makes problems worse in the long run by offering a short-term fix. We need smaller government. We need a recession to rebalance the phony economy. But the recession is a bitter medicine, the sooner we take it, the better our economy will be.

Robbing Peter to Pay Paul

The concept of social security was originally sold to the public as an insurance program. The idea was our government pooled part of everyone's earnings to create a security net for people in need. This sound like a good thing, but there is only one problem. Our social security account is going to go bankrupt.

Believe it or not, the whole idea of Social Security is a giant Ponzi scheme. The money contributed by people generations ago is not there anymore, it was all spent by government generations ago! The social security checks collected by the older generation today were not what was contributed years ago. These are actually collected from young people through payroll tax today. Recently I read a prediction which stated that social benefits alone will cost the government half of its budget during this decade! It becomes a fiscal cancer. The government can cut whatever spending they like but not social security. Cutting this will downgrade their report card from 'A' to 'F' instantaneously. So in order to protect this Ponzi scheme, the government fleeces young generations to contribute a higher percentage of our wages into social security. This ensures that older generations continuously gets their check to proove that social security is financially healthy. But do you think that generations today will get the same benefits as the current older generations? I doubt it. If we do, then our children will have to contribute far more from their wages to keep the ponzi scheme alive. This can't last forever, but only time will tell.

Socialism Does Not Work?

In fact, the great economist, Ludwig Von Mises already proved the impossibility of economic calculation under socialism. Social security does not work and will never work. The reason for that is because the government ignores market price and efficiency. The government thinks that the hands of the state have better management than the free market.

The results of government decisions discourage everyone from working hard, it makes it become meaningless for entrepreneurs to take risks. The end result is reducing the economic means and the efficiency of the market. The substituted decisions become socially irrational, uneconomical and sometimes political chaotic. I will show you a simple example of Mises's theorem.

Suppose we are going to accomplish a task. It requires capital goods (M) and labor (L). These are the inputs to produce a product. Altogether, we come up with three different methods and each has these own input levels.

Method	Requires to Accomplish a Task	
	Unit of Capital Goods Required (M)	Unit of Labor Required (L)
A	2	10
B	4	6
C	8	3

The time required to produce these capital goods is t_0 and t_1. The cost of production for each timeframe is summarized below.

Time Required	Price per unit Input	
T_0	$P_M=\$4$	$P_L=\$1$
T_1	$P_M=\$3$	$P_L=\$2$

Now, how can we economize our resources consumption to accomplish a given task?

Free Market Approach

Under the free market, different methods have different costs. As an entrepreneur, we have to find the way to minimize the cost of production to maximize profits.

If we want to finish the product by T_0

Total cost of production of method A = P_m x M + P_L x L

$$= \$4 \text{ x } 2 + \$1 \text{ x } 10$$
$$= \$18$$

Total cost of production of method B = P_m x M + P_L x L

$$= \$4 \text{ x } 4 + \$1 \text{ x } 6$$
$$= \$22$$

Total cost of production of method C = P_m x M + P_L x L

$$= \$4 \text{ x } 8 + \$1 \text{ x } 3$$
$$= \$35$$

So Method A will be the optimum way to produce the product as it has the lowest cost of production. Let's see what happen if we want to finish the product by T_1

Total cost of production of method A = P_m x M + P_L x L

$$= \$3 \text{ x } 2 + \$2 \text{ x } 10$$
$$= \$26$$

Total cost of production of method B = P_m x M + P_L x L

$$= \$3 \text{ x } 4 + \$2 \text{ x } 6$$
$$= \$24$$

Total cost of production of method C = P_m x M + P_L x L

$$= \$3 \text{ x } 8 + \$2 \text{ x } 3$$
$$= \$30$$

Now method B will be a more economical approach. So you see capitalism has a self adjustment mechanism. Everyone will go for the lowest cost of production. What about the government approach?

Government Approach

Under the government approach, the story is very different. There are no method A, method B nor method C. There are no T_0 nor T_1 either. The government can use any of these methods to accomplish a task. Instead of making an economical decision like an entrepreneur, politicians base these decisions on their own beliefs. These decisions are always based on emotions and abstract ideas which are right in their own sense but not in economical calculations.

In U.S.,the annual book titled "Wastebook" by Senator Coburn lists all sorts of the way that the government wastes the taxpayer's money. Some of the examples are very unbelievable!

Studying World of Warcraft and Other Virtual Games -*In 2008, Professor Bonnie Nardi of the University of California-Irvine received $100,007 from the National Science Foundation to —analyze and understand the ways in which players of World of Warcraft, a popular multiplayer game, engage in creative collaboration.*   **-WasteBook 2010**

Internet Dating Study – *The National Science Foundation directed nearly a quarter of a million dollars to Stanford University professor's study of how American use Internet to find love.*   **-WasteBook 2010**

Can Social Security Continue Forever?

"Ching, if you ever played musical chairs before, what happened when the music was over?"

"Everyone must race to sit down in one of the chairs. The player who is left without a chair is eliminated from the game."

"I predict that the music of social security will soon come to an end. Later generations like yours or your children are going to be eliminated from the game."

"But how do you know. We have all contributed to it, haven't we? People have paid 7.5% of their income into social security, and they believed they would get it back."

"This is what they are told to believe." Grandad smiled.

My Grandad is an employer, and he knew tax law by heart.

"By law, both the employer and the employee need to contribute 7.5% each to payroll tax (PAYG or social security) and we did. But do you think an employer will take it out of their profit?"

"Huh, do you mean the employer will contribute it from somewhere else?"

"Indeed. This cost is passed to the employees even before they noticed."

"How do they do it?"

"They do it by reducing your salary. So instead of earning $50,000, your salary package will be $46,250. The net amount goes to the company's social security tax. Another 7.5% will be taxed on the remaining $46,250."

"But that's unfair!"

"The most unfair part is that by your retirement age. All your life's contribution in social society may not provide you with social security. Because to do that, the payroll tax must increase to 20% or 25%. Will you or future generations put up with that?"

Ring Finger: Healthcare

Once I accompanied grandad for a body check up in a government healthcare centre. He asked the doctors what does it costs to do these particular tests. Not one doctor could or would answer. After a while, one reply was " Why do you have to care about the cost? You are not the one who is paying for it. "

What is the Cost of Health Care?

Do you know health care is the fastest growing cost today? In Australia, the health expenditures increased to $121.4 billion in 2009-2010, which is 9.4% of GDP and rising. The government funded 89.9% of these health expenditure from taxation or other revenues. In other words, you and I are paying for it. Are you using very much healthcare this year?

In some countries the Medicare levy is collected through payroll tax from the employee and employers. The employer and employee both pay 7.5% each. It may sound like a great deal to begin with when you first heard that your employer is paying for your health benefit too. But it is the same drama as social security. There is no such thing as a free lunch.

But What is the Good Side of it?

The government tries to make things attractive by offering it tax benefits. So the idea is that instead of people paying it with their after-tax money, the government mandates people to pay for their healthcare with their earnings before tax.

Does Health Insurance Make Any Sense?

Because of the skyrocketing cost in health care, recently government mandated medium income earner to pay a proportion of their income to buy health insurance. Wait a minute, does health insurance make any sense to you? My Grandad never had health insurance and he lived to the age of 82. Think about what insurance is. It makes sense to buy fire insurance "*just in case*" a disaster happens and our house burns down. People buy life insurance and car insurance for the same purpose. People buy insurance because of low probability damage and high cost of replacement. The premium collected from this "*just in case*" mentality is how insurance companies make profit. So what about health insurance?

Will you insure against flu or a paper cut in the office? No one will do that. So this makes people to use insurance they normally wouldn't insure for, thus sending healthcare costs even higher.

Shouldn't Health Care be Cheaper with Better Technology?

We have all this cutting edge medical equipment which was not available in the past. This medical equipment is often very expensive to use. That's why it should be expensive. Does that sound logical to you?

But if you rethink for a second, why shouldn't better technology drive usage prices down? Almost all technology goods like computers, plasma TV's, go down in price. Every year they are becoming more powerful, and every year they are become more and more affordable. Why isn't this happening to health care? The reason lies in the involvement from government.

How Does the Government Make Health Care More Expensive?

The result of Government involvement in Medicare business is that anyone who paid for Medicare levy can basically abuse the services. Why not? After all, we paid for it. It is our right to get most out of our medicare levy, right? The problem is that this creates more health care demand than it normally would. Higher demand drives the price higher.

When you go shopping, you will see the price tag of things. When Mary's cosmetic company costs $100 to do a facial but Vicky's beauty shop costs only $90. Provided they have the same quality of services, people will prefer Vicky's beauty centre over Mary's. This forces Mary to reduce her price. People don't have price sensitivity when it comes to health care. That's why sometimes you'll see even doctors do not know how much it costs to provide the services they provide daily. Getting the government to be a third party payer in healthcare is an absurd idea. It will only make health care become more expensive for everybody.

Health Care Without Government

Right now it is difficult to remove healthcare and social security completely because we have a generation or two dependent on it. But we cannot continue to head down this road either. Today health care is an even a greater problem than social security. In U.S., healthcare is most likely to be the first social program to go bankrupt by the end of this decade.

Like everything else, without government involvement, healthcare costs could go down. If you have a look at eye laser surgery, it is not part of health insurance coverage or Medicare program, it requires high cost equipment, it is run by private doctors, and through competition, it becomes more and more affordable.

Unfortunately those people in charge to help solve the healthcare problems are the very people who worsen it. The problem is that they do not realize it. Increasing the payroll tax and enforcing health insurance will not help to bring the cost down in the long term, it will only make it more expensive.

Little Finger: Employment

If you read a single political statement, it is impossible not to hear the word jobs dozen of times- *"jobs, jobs, jobs"*. Jobs are important. Most people need jobs to make a living. Government needs jobs to grow the economy. In fact, everyone should keep an hawk eye on unemployment statistics as an indicator to of the health of our economy. They believe that the government can help the economy by creating more jobs. They are wrong. Jobs may not be the solution to recession. It depends what type of jobs created. In fact, government should not be involved in the job creation business at all.

What is the Purpose of Jobs?

Like the concept of money. The concept of jobs is invented by the free market. It was created out of need. In Agrarian age, the economy was simple. Everyone was self employed. The only job for a person was to specialize in a skill such that no other could provide for him to make a profit. It doesn't matter whether it was hunting, tool making, crop growing or fishing. Everyone was self employed. There was no such thing as unemployment.

As society became more complex, people started to work for others by trading their labor for wages. For a job to exist, there must be an employer or at least one employee. The wage of the job was set by the amount an employee is willing to accept and an employer is willing to pay. This wage is set by the free market. The whole purpose of job is to help the employer (entrepreneur) to make profits which would be impossible without the value of the labor input from the employee. The result of profits made from these jobs caused the economy to expand.

Can Government Really Create Real Jobs?

Not all jobs can grow the economy. Only real jobs do. An example of real jobs will be Company A who employs workers, invests their capital and turns raw materials into products like electric motors, and then sells them for a profit. These jobs are productive. They grow the economy because the motors sold help with the mining of natural resources. They increase the efficiency of production lines.These are what I mean by 'real jobs'. Government jobs are still jobs, but the profits made from these jobs cannot cause the economy to expand. For example, hospitals, police stations or fire stations are providing services to the public sector. They still create values to the economy and government employees still earn wages. But if you look at the entire picture, these government created jobs are created out of tax to provide services back to the private sector. These jobs cannot earn money for the employer, the government, and therefore cannot contrbute profits. It is just a redistribution of resources. More of these jobs will only dry up tax revenues. Next time when you see the government spend a lot of money on job creations but the economy is still firmly in a recession, you can advise the government what is happening!

I am Here for Small Businesses

Every politician says they are all for small businesses. I have never seen a politician on stage who is not stating that they support small businesses. But, despite what they promise, they are actually killing the small businesses. Does the government understand how business works? I often wonder. Government revenues are derived from taxes. Entrepreneur's profit is derived from taking risks. It is ironic that government imposes such a lot of taxes and regulations on companies yet says they support small businesses. These policies only makes it riskier for an entrepreneur to take the necessary risks. If it turns out to be unprofitable, no real jobs are created. It is important to have regulations, but too many regulations kill jobs. That's why unemployment stays so high.

Hiring is very expensive. There are a lot of costs involved. One of them is payroll tax. It can either be a deduction from employee wages (PAYG) or tax paid by the employer based on employee wages. Payroll tax is used to fund social security, unemployment insurance or other social benefits.

This tax is in advance of the income tax. So no matter what, an employee will never see this money end up in their pocket. Like any taxes, this tax puts unnecessary risk for small businesses to hire, it hurts the employee and discourages job creation.

Mystery of Minimum Wage

Making profits is already difficult. These profits are firstly eroded by tax and regulations, then goes to pay the employee before anything ends up in the employer's pocket. Remember the purpose of employers is to make a profit and ultimately creates jobs. The profit is what drives a person to run a business. So employee wages should be dependent on how much productivity is contributed by the individual helping to make that profit. In other words, the wage is decided by the Free Market. Competent will be paid more and incompetent will be paid less. The employer has any right to fire the incompetents that hinder the business to make a profit. In reality, the government thinks it is not good for the economy as it creates unemployment. So what the government does is that it imposes a law called 'the minimum wage', which is set by the government, not the free market. Every employer must at least pay the minimum wage. What do you think will happen? Will the employer really paid the minimum wage? They won't. The result of the minimum wage is that the employer will get rid of all the jobs below the minimum wage value. Any jobs that were initially higher than the minimum wage will now be set to or just slightly above the minimum wage level. The result - more unemployment.

Why Government Solutions Never Work?

So you see the government can never solve the long term problems, whether it is housing, employment, healthcare, social security or education. Even with noble intentions, they will only worsen the social problems in the long run by getting involved. So what went wrong? I give you an analogy to think about. This is borrowed from *Milton Friedman's* idea to demonstrate why welfare state doesn't work. I call it the *Spending Quadrant*. Each quadrant tells differently how you value money when it comes to spending.

You are the Spender

On Whom Spent

Whose Money	You	SomeoneElse
Yours	A	B
Someone Else's	C	D

In category A, you are using your money and spend it on yourself. These are your hard earned money. Remember the last time you buy something or book for holiday? You will certainly get the best value of every dollar you spend.

In category B, you are spending your money on someone else. For example, you are buying a gift for your boss or for your mother's birthday. You will still spend time to shop for something they like. But when you compare this with Category A, you will most likely not have the same incentive, time and drive to get the full value of the dollar.

Category C refers to you spending someone else's money on yourself. For example, you are being sponsored by your company for a holiday trip overseas, you will probably have no intentions to keep the cost down. It is a free lunch after all, but you will still get the best value of the money you spend.

Category D refers to you spending someone else's money on someone else. You will have the least incentive to think carefully how the money is spent, let alone to consider maximizing the spending to its full value. This is the most wasteful and inefficient way of spending among all four categories. Ironically, this model is how the government spend our taxes today.

All government welfares fall on either category C or category D. When you vote for someone to be in office, whether it is the republicans or democrats, you are more likely to vote them to have policies which favor you. Very rarely you are voting for someone to tax you more. Under such arrangement, do you see why all our government social programs are skyrocketing?

In fact, if you interview social welfare receivers and ask them about their benefits, most of them will reply that it is insufficient. But if you interview ten middle class, most of them will agree they pay enough tax on social security already. So what is missing here?

According to research on *The University of New South Wales,* approximately 2.2 million people, roughly 11% of the Australian population is living in poverty. If the entire welfare budget is given to the poor, the average poor people can have an entitlement of $59,818 AUD or $239,272 AUD for a family of four without doing anything. However, the average income in Australia is around $46,500 (2008-09 data). If that $59,818 AUD is really given to the poor, then they will be among the rich. This money given to them will put them in the top 20% of the distribution. But in reality this money is not really given to the poor, it is given to people entitled to get the social security check even if they are not poor. Since the middle class has the largest proportion in the society, most of these money are flowing back to them , maybe flowing back to people like you and me.

Another thing is that, suppose the total payroll tax collected is X amount, when it goes through the government and pays welfare authorities to regulate, legislate and hold welfare campaigns, the net amount will always be less than X. That's why we don't need bigger government.

Lesson 12:

Whenever our government get involves in social issues, whether it is education, housing, social security, healthcare or employment, be expect the cost to skyrocket.

When our government redistributes resources from the competents to the incompetents, the result is the slow down of economic growth. Borrowing from the future and spend it today will only make things much more costly in the future. This is the true meaning of Robin Hood of the 21st century.

Chapter 6

My Time Travel on Real Money

"The farther backward you can look, the farther forward you are likely to see."
-Winston Churchill

I will never forget Charles Dickens' opening paragraph on his famous book – *A Tale of Two Cities*.

> *It was the best of times, it was the worst of times,*
> *it was the age of wisdom, it was the age of foolishness,*
> *it was the epoch of belief, it was the epoch of incredulity,*
> *it was the season of Light, it was the season of Darkness,*
> *it was the spring of hope, it was the winter of despair,*
> *we had everything before us, we had nothing before us,*
> *we were all going direct to Heaven, we were all going direct the other*
> *way*

Over the years, Grandad had reflected upon this paragraph of the novel to me. His philosophy is that there is no such thing as good times or bad times. It depends on whether you have positioned yourself in the right side of the equation. While others say the economy was bad doesn't have to mean it was bad for you. In fact, it can be the exact opposite. He was right. In 1980, the world had a very bad recession. Inflation was ragging. Unemployment went double digits. Currency was a doomed place to be. Within a couple of months, gold accelerated up to $850 per ounce. Grandad was consistently buying it from $35 per ounce in the entire decade and exited around the top. He had been guiding me through the bull market. I made a handsome gain and became the richest kid in my class. It was all pre-planned. Shortly afterwards, the Federal Reserve Chairman Paul Volcker was forced to make a critical decision to combat inflation. He increased the interest rate all the way up to 20%. Gold plummeted afterwards. He successfully killed the inflation at the expense of sacrificing the housing market. Foreclosures were everywhere. My dad was earning 20% interest of his money in the bank. Grandad entered the real estate market while everyone try to get rid of it. It was the best of the times for him, it was the worst of the times for others. When I asked how Grandad knew Gold is going to skyrocket. His answer was *"He seen in before, it is just history repeating."*

It is Just History Repeating

If you have ever taken an exam in high school or university, you probably know what past papers were. The more past papers you do, the more confident you feel and the better grades you get at exams, right? This chapter will study some past papers of money. We called it monetary history. It is probably one of the most important chapter in this book. Studying monetary history is like studying past exam papers. If you study what had happened in the past, you will have a higher chance to predict accurately what will happen in the future. It is just history repeating with a twist. To understand monetary history, the best starting point is to understand what is happening to our currency.

The World Reserve Currency

When you are reading this book at the moment, the U.S. Dollar should still be the *world reserve currency*. But what is â world reserve currency? It is a currency most widely use for commerce. It is a currency held by many governments as a foreign exchange reserve. It is a currency businesses use for daily transactions. In fact if you put all the world currency into a basket, you will see that U.S. dollar dominates the entire foreign exchange market. It has a share of 62%. Euro has a share of 24%. Other currencies play a very insignificant role in the foreign exchange market.

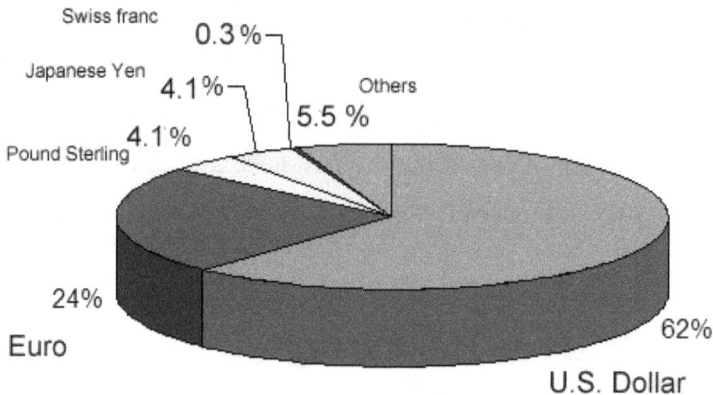

Swiss franc 0.3%
Japanese Yen 4.1%
Others 5.5 %
Pound Sterling 4.1 %
24%
Euro
62%
U.S. Dollar

Chart 6.1 Global Reserve Currency in 2012 Q3

This chart tells a story why U.S. dollar is so important today. It represents a large portion of all the world's currencies. If U.S. dollar catches a cold, the world will get sick. If you look at what is happening to the world economy today, this time around, I suspect the U.S. dollar has cancer.

Can Renminbi Replace U.S. Dollar?

Not long ago, I was listening to a Radio show debate about which currency is going to replace U.S. dollar as the next world reserve currency. The question was like this.

Which is the next World Reserve Currency?

1   Australian Dollar

2   Chinese Renminbi

3   Euro

4   Canadian Dollar

While both the host and the guest in the show vote for *Renminbi* because Chinese has the 2nd biggest economy in the world, it is the global economic powerhouse. Most of the things we buy today are made in China. On the surface, their logic can potentially make sense. China is currently holding most of the world's resources, in addition to the trillions of dollar of foreign reserves. It is where wealth and business are flowing now and in the future. There is no doubt Chinese *Renminbi* will be the next U.S. dollar.

But if you look at the share of global reserve currency, *Renminbi* makes up of less than 5.5% of the world reserve currency in the foreign exchange market. In China, the government is trying very hard to combat the ragging inflation. Some cities have real estate price gone up to 7 or 8 digits. If you ask any local Chinese and you will realize their living expense is going through the roof. But what does inflation has to do with being the world reserve currency? By having a second look at the chart on global reserve currency, you will understand the picture. If Chinese *Renminbi* becomes the world reserve currency, that means demand of *Renminbi* has to go up. *Renminbi* must have a larger currency market share no smaller than U.S dollar. In other words, the Chinese government will have to print multiple times the existing *Renminbi*. The worse case scenario is hyperinflation and renders *Renminbi* worthless.

U.S Dollar is As Good as Gold

"Grandad, how do you know gold price will skyrocket?" I asked curiously. Obviously I don't take luck as an answer because it clearly wasn't. It was more like a plan.

Grandad smiled and wrote down a few words on a piece of paper.

U.S. Dollar <u>was</u> as good as Gold

You, as a diligent reader, probably would have heard of similar phase from people in the 70s or 80s. Why do people accept the U.S dollar as the world reserve currency? There is a story behind this.

Gold has been used as money for more than 5,000 years. It is chosen as money by the free market. Its rarity is what creates its value. Unlike paper currency, the government cannot print gold out of thin air. Gold needs to be minted. So every year the world has a steady and predictable amount of gold added to the market. If we are purely using gold as our money supply, the increasing gold supply will still cause inflation, but it is going to be mild and steady. If you have relatives lived thought the 50s or 60s. This was exactly what happened. Prices were much more stable compared with today. People might not earn as much income as we do now, but the purchasing power of their currencies were maintained. Back then the U.S. dollar as the world reserve currency was backed by Gold. One U.S. dollar was pegged to Gold at $35 per ounce. All the other world currencies were pegged to U.S. dollar. Everyone in the world knew gold was money. With U.S. dollar playing as the role of Gold, U.S. dollar was as good as gold.

Lesson 13:

If we use Gold as money, we will have a steady economic growth. We might have a delay of having the level of prosperity like we have today, but the economy will be less volatile. Under a gold back currency system, the money supply is inelastic. Under a fiat currency system, we are living at the age of turbulence. the government and monetary authority can expand our money supply at will. By doing so, we enjoyed an unprecedented prosperity the world ever lived. But this will not go on forever, someday the borrowed prosperity will be repaid.

The Magic of Gold as Monetary Asset

The reason Grandad bought gold was not because he bet on Gold going up in prices. He bought Gold because he saw that the government was making all the wrong political decisions and tried to manipulate the economy. The more they try to cheat gold, the more gold will re-valuate.

Gold is not an investment. It is money. Its role is to rebalance the economy. Amazingly it has a self adjustment mechanism built in by the free market, not by people. To understand how gold works as a monetary asset, I have an example.

Suppose U.S. and China are using Gold as money. For the sake of simplicity, each country starts off with 1000oz of gold in their account. When China trades with U.S., she exports goods she produces and imports things she needs. When China exports more than she imports, then China is in trade surplus. In this case when U.S. imports more goods she produces, then she has to pay gold to China. So in U.S., there will be less gold circulated in the country. The outflow of Gold will cause the U.S. economy to contract. This contraction will cause a recession. Business will have to cut employees and reduce the price through competitions. The free market will readjust the price of goods until it reaches a point where the U.S. becomes trade competitive again. Then Gold will flow back to U.S. On the other hand; China will have an economic boom as gold inflow into the country. Too much gold chasing after goods will cause inflation. Price of goods and services will become expensive locally. This reduces China trade competitiveness. Export will decline, and China will rely on importing goods from U.S. Gold will then outflow back to U.S. from China. This cycle repeats itself. This is how Gold works as a monetary asset. The government plays no role at all during this process. This adjustment is automatic. The idea is to prevent trade imbalance.

Every time governments believe they can substitute gold by their monetary policies, Inevitable financial disasters happen. It had happened in the past, and it will happen in the future.

Fall of Athens – The Greatest Civilization

"Throughout history, civilizations rise and fall. Wealth of nations comes and goes. A pattern has been repeating like the law of nature. History is full of examples of greed leading a populace to do incredible stupid things and causes boom and bursts of the economy. These economic cycles can be a disaster or a gift. Now you have earned your first fortune, it is time for you to understand why it happens." Grandad spoke as we walked to his library.

"Grandad, I remembered the last time you told me that gold and silver are chosen by the free market as money. The concept of gold and silver as money form the foundation of coinage. Civilizations flourished once they substituted other commodities with gold and silver for commerce. It became like a magic formula to prosperity."

"Yes it is. The first experiment in human history was carried out in Athens, the greatest civilization of all times. The earliest form of coinage as money was dated back in Lydia around the fifth century B.C. The Lydians were the first ones who use Gold and Silver as coinage. "

"Why is the Athens the greatest civilization of all times?"

"Back then, people already understand money should be defined in weight. Coins are minted in equal weight of different denominations. This makes trade easier. According to Greek historian *Herodotus*, Lydians were recorded as the first merchant who has a free market transition from agricultural barter economy to an urban economy using gold and silver coins for commerce. "

Grandad picked up one of the books on self to show me the photos of Lydian coins.

Source: Author

"In order to maintain the coins scarcity, the law was very strict. Solons of Athens announced that anyone who debases the coin – including himself – will have his hands chop off. Because of the sound money system, Athens flourished. Because of the integrity of the monetary system, the Athenians "owl" was a widely accepted currency for six centuries. Athens shone brightly. If you have studied history lessons, you will know that Athens was one of the greatest civilizations."

"Yes. I did learn that. But even Athens was powerful, it eventually felt, right? Who defeated her?"

"Athens was a very powerful nation indeed. Her power threatened many nearby countries. This inevitably engaged herself in many wars. As times pass, it turned out that the war was more expensive and lasted much longer than expected. The Athens was running out of money. In order to fund the war, the Athenians though of an idea."

"What is it?"

"Deficit spending" Grandad smiled. "Unlike what is happening today, where the Federal Reserve debases our currency supply by creating currency out of thin air, the Athens did not have a printing press. If you are the Athens, how would you debase the coins?"

"Umm…can coins be debased? I thought only paper currency can be created with no limit. Coins need to be minted. It has a fixed supply. We cannot create more coins out of thin air"

"Strangely enough they can."

"But how?"

"The Athens mixed their money with base metals like copper. Then they can produce more coins to fight the war. For example, if you take 10,000 gold and silver coins, mix them with 50% copper content, and then stamp them with the same weight content. You will now have 20,000 coins. When the government enforces them to be legal tender, few people will notice that as the government gradually dilutes their currency supply. Coins are becoming lighter with less and less value."

"I see. I guess in the end; there are too many coins in circulation. People are holding more coins than ever but they cannot buy much."

"Eventually the economy of Athens collapsed. The rest is history. People who were holding physical gold and silver maintained or even increased their purchasing power."

"Wow. Sounds like what just happened to us." I exclaimed.

The Rise and Fall of Rome

"But may Athens be a special case?" I questioned.

"Athens is just one of the few examples in history. Many history books recorded Rome prosperity was eroded by war, corruption and greed of merchants. There are some truths to them. But this was not the main reason why Rome falls."

"Really? I though the assassination of Julius Caesar marked the beginning of downfall of Rome."

"Do you know how Julius Caesar became the icon of Rome apart from his brilliant in politics and military?"

"I have no idea Grandad."

"During Caesar's career, he noticed that for Rome to expand and prosper, they must have a sound economy. Julius Caesar adopted a hard money standard. All the coins issued by the government had a fixed proportion of gold content. Because of a sound monetary foundation, Rome's commerce flourished, many industries began to develop. Roman republic transformed into Roman Empire. The wealth of nations began."

"But if the gold standard was so powerful, how did Rome felt apart? It was a very powerful nation indeed."

"Due to war, the Roman empire expanded at an accelerating pace. As their military cost increases, so did their demand for Gold. In fact, the Romans were always facing a constant problem of not enough gold. So the Roman Empire was left with three choices. The first choice was to live with the fact of not enough gold. But the price was to suffer economic crisis. The second choice was to import more gold abroad or simply dig more out of the ground. The third option was the easiest and least headache. They simply debased their currency supply. If you were in control, which option will you choose?"

"Option three. It gave me the least headache."

"Exactly. So what they did over the years was that emperors debased the currency supply. Coins minted had the same face value but felt lighter with less metal content. At the beginning, the public did not notice it. But the problem is that you can fool people sometimes, you cannot fool people all the time. By the time *Diocletian* became the emperor, Roman coinage were nothing more than tin-plated copper or bronze."

"So what brought down Roman Empire is not war but inflation."

"You got it. Back then there were already price controls by the government to suppress inflation. Emperor *Diocletian* issued *Edict on Maximum Price* in 310 A.D. to combat the ragging inflation. In the last third of the Edict, *Diocletian* fixed price of almost 1,000 of the products. This included beef, fish, grains, eggs and clothing etc. Wages were also one of them. They even imposed death penalty on those who attempted to raise price."

"Did price control works? The Roman government was trying to rearrange the economy like what is happening today."

"It turns out that price control was not effective at all. It only worsens the situation. Eventually merchants cannot make a profit and closed down the shop. Farmers cannot make a profit and therefore, left the farms. The end game is hyperinflation and the Roman currency collapsed. People returned back to barter. The Dark age began."

"But there must be someone owning Gold coins instead of the tin-plated copper ones."

"History shown that Roman *denarius* had fallen 30,000,000:1 from its value under *Augustus*. According to history, this means gold price rose 42,400 times in less than 50 years. To put it into today's perspective. If we take gold at $850/oz at the base, a 42,400 fold will mean gold will reach $36,040,000/oz."

"$36,040,000 per ounce! Isn't this insane?"

"Yes I know. This is how crazy it can get when the currency collapses. Roman greed of conquer led to overexpansion in military. The expense of war was a shortage of money. The result was debasement of their money supply and destroys the currency. The fall of Rome was no more than another episode of greed and war."

Who Invent Paper Currency?

"Ching, we are all using paper currency today. But where is the origin of this idea in the first place?"

"Was it the Federal Reserve in U.S?"

"No. The Fed was created in 1913. We had paper currency way before that."

"Oh yes, you are right. Was it Europe?"

"No. Ironically it is a product of China."

"China?"

"It was Marco Polo, the great merchant traveller and his uncles, brought the concept of paper currency and printing press back to Europe in the 13th century. In his book, *The Travel of Marco Polo*, he described paper currency as *flying money* because the money could just fly from your hand."

"I knew him. That's where my name came from!"

Why Banks are called Silver Movement?

"But was paper currency any success?" I asked curiously.

"The problem of inflation haunted China since the birth of paper currency. In the 14th century, Mongol was suffering deep devaluation of their currency. Like Rome, their economy collapsed, and citizens were forced to return to barter system. Ming Dynasty upraise and attempted to revive paper currency. They never succeed as the currency continued to lose value rapidly. This was when silver comes into play."

"Silver?"

"Silver had a close relationship with China. By 1455, Ming government officially disconnected paper currency from their economy and introduced silver as money. As the population grew, the demand of silver also grew. The introduction of metallic silver standard caused the demand of silver to skyrocket. China needed an unprecedented amount of silver to facilitate commerce. So huge amount of silver were traded with Europe, Japan and other countries in the southern hemisphere."

"Oh I begin to understand why Chinese banks are named this way…"

"Yes. Because silver was used as money and it needed to be transported from one place to another for commerce. Banks were the issuer of money. So that's why today's Chinese banks literally mean silver movement for this reason. Ming economy suffered when silver coins were debased during 1620. Silver supply was cut from its trading partners. Eventually, Ming Dynasty economy collapsed just like any others."

Holland Tulip Fantasy

Will you pay $1 million for a single Tulip? This is not a joke. This is a true story. No fantasy. When people think of tulip, most of us will think of Holland. Surprisingly, tulips were not originally from Holland. In 1593, they were brought from Turkey and then introduced into Holland.

But how do tulips relate to money? The key is scarcity. Tulips were very different from other known plants in Europe. They exhibit a saturated intense petal color that no other plants match. To a flowering bulb from seeds, they take 7-12 years. If a tulip is properly cultivated, it will produce a single color. But if it is infected by a virus, it will have a breaking pattern which makes it a very scarce commodity. Because of rarity, tulips become precious. They quickly become a status symbol of wealth and royalty. Later on, a tulip exchange was set up for trading.

Speculators bit up the price of these infected tulips, and the price rose rapidly. It doesn't take long until the madness of the crowd all rushes into tulips. To give you an idea how crazy the speculations were. Let's look at some price of goods to exchange for a tulip. During that period, a skilled labor earned 150*f* (florins) a year. The exchange for a single tulip was 2500*f*.

Exchange for a single Tulip	
Two Last of wheat	448ƒ
Four lasts of rye	558ƒ
Four fat oxen	480ƒ
Eight fat swine	240ƒ
Twelve fat sheep	120ƒ
Two hogheads of wine	70ƒ
Four tuns of beer	32ƒ
Two tons of butter	192ƒ
1,000 lb of cheese	120ƒ
A complete bed	100ƒ
A suit of clothes	80ƒ
A silver drinking cup	60ƒ
Total	2,500ƒ

In 1637, tulip mania reached its peak, it was reported that some tulip changed hands 10 times per day. The price rose by 1000% in one year! One record setting tulip bulb, *the Semper Augustus*, sold for 6,000ƒ. This is 40 times the average wages! If you put it into today's perspective, the average salary for a full time job in Australia is around $69,592. That means a single tulip will cost you $2,783,680! Will you pay that much for a flower? I hope not except maybe during the valentine day.

John Law Roller Coaster Tycoon

Winston Churchill once said the farther backward you can look, the farther forward you are likely to see. The inflation we are experiencing today is nothing unprecedented like most financial experts said in media. It had happened in the past, and it will happen again in the future.

Perhaps the life story of John Law is a proper example to explain this. Law's life can be best described as an adventure of currency creation. His life was a roller coaster ride.

Law was born in a family of the banker and goldsmith in Scotland. He was a genius in many areas like mathematics, commerce and economy. He had a bright future. Unfortunately, instead of using his genius for the goods, he grew up as a gambler and a lover boy. He lost almost all his family fortune in gambling. Even worse, he fought a duel with his opponent called Wilson over a woman and killed him with a thrust of his sword. He was arrested, charged for murder. With some luck, his sentence was commuted to fine only. Later on Wilson's brother appealed and had Law kept in prison. Law escaped and fled to France.

Ten years later, Law returned back to Scotland and wrote a Book called *Money and Trade Considered with a Proposal for Supplying Nation with Money (1705)* and began promoting his idea on national banking. He travelled around Europe to promote his idea. The sad thing was that no one listened to him.

Coincidentally, France was on the edge of bankrupt due to war. *Duke d'Orleans* was a temporary king at that moment after the death of *Louis XIV.* He watched as the country went deeper and deeper into debt, and taxes were not even enough to cover his interest payment. He was desperate for a solution. Law saw a golden opportunity. He presented himself to *Duke d'Orleans.*

"Your Majesty, the solution is simple. There are simply not enough money around. All we need is to introduce paper currencies."

On May 20 1976, Law was granted a license to establish a bank (*'Banque Générale*) in France and given the right to print paper currencies as a receipt of Gold.

Amazingly it works! *'Banque Générale* was very successful at running a paper currency scheme. Later on, the currency Law issued becomes the official currency of France. It seems that France can finally be relieved from their financial trouble. Law was granted as a financial genius. He became the minister of finance.

Duke d'Orleans rewarded Law by granting him the right and power to exploit the *Mississippi* regions and trade from *Louisiana* territory. It was a big gift because *Louisiana* was a very wealthy piece of land, rich in gold. Later on, he brought *Mississippi* company, which became an investment company. Law consolidated many of his rivals. To put it into today's perspective, he is as powerful as the Federal Reserve Chairman today. If you think about it, Law was initially a gambler, a murderer waiting to be hang in, and end up being the most powerful banker known all across Europe. His life was truly a roaster coaster ride.

Law was the ultimate architect of the infamous *Mississippi* bubble. He exaggerated the wealth of Louisiana and encouraged speculations of his *Mississippi* company. Because people demanded more paper currency to buy shares, the result was that Law had to issue a gigantic amount of banknotes. Millions of paper notes inflated the stock price. So whenever new shares were issued, Law's house would be sieged. Every morning, people would queue up and wait for the trade. The stock market became a get-rich-quick platform. One day a guy is a plumber, and the next day he might be a prince. In just a few months, *Mississippi* shares value increased over 30 times.

It all went well until one day, when a wealthy prince demanded his gold for all his paper currency and his *Mississippi* stock. The truth was exposed. There was only enough gold to match one-fifth of the currency supply. As words spread, the public rushed to the banks to redeem their gold. *Duke d'Orleans* and Law tried different policies to stop the gold rush but everything they tried failed. They needed to close down the banks. The situation was out of control.

The *Mississippi* bubble burst at the end of 1720. Law dismissed from France by disguising as a woman. He returned back to his normal life of gambling. There was a famous saying by John Law while he was drunk.

"Last year I was the wealthiest person who has ever lived, today I have nothing." Law died broke in the end.

Lesson 14:

By going back through times and look at some of the examples throughout history. You have probably figured out the lessons are quite repetitive, and they all end the same way. Whenever an emperor, a nation or a country debases its currency through deficit spending. The currency is always self-destructive.

The Battle that Never Ends

"Ching, so that's why I said I have seen in before. History keeps on repeating itself. The battle between currency and real money will continue now and in the future. It is a battle that never ends. Whenever a government tries to debase their currency, gold and everything else will revaluate themselves as the public wakes up, and catch up with all the currencies that have been produced. Ironically politicians never seems to understand this."

"It is only not the quantity of money which is important, but the quality as well."

"You got it."

Chapter 7

Why an Economy Grows and Why it Crashes?

Before the rise of United States, England was the world great power. There had been a saying that the sun never sets on British flag. The British Empire occupied many places around the world. There was at least one territory in daylight. British pound was once the world's reserve currency.

Wealth of Nations

Throughout history, wealth of nations never lasts. It migrates from one country to another then another. In the early 20th Century, it shifted from Great Britain to U.S., today the wealth is in transit from U.S. to China. We are feeling that more every day. Right? But what causes that to happen? How does a nation rise and fall? Why does an economy grows and then why it crashes?

A Hypothesis of Labor Based Economy

Before the 19th century, the world was very different from today. About 80% of the world population was in Agrarian economy. It was agricultural based. Food and clothing sum up to a lot of average household expenditures. Global GDP was very low. If you want to visualize what it was like, think about what the world would be without modern transportations, without instant communications, without energy, without factories to manufacture goods. Everything we did were labor based. You can imagine things will go much slower. The economic output will be very low.

To put that into perspective today how labor based economy works, let's go back in time before there was electricity. As I am writing now, my average electricity usage is 7.44kWh (kilo Watts per hour). I need 7.44kW per hour to enjoy the lifestyle I am enjoying today. This power will cost me an average of $2.04 per day. A healthy cyclist can generate electricity of 200Watts per hour by cycling non-stop. So that means in order for me to sustain the same level of lifestyle I am enjoying, it takes about 38 of these cyclists to exercise continuously. Is it possible to hire 38 cyclists for $2.04 per day. Even if I pay $20/hr per cyclist to do this exercise, I still need to pay $760 just to fund my one hour of electricity usage. This assumes no cyclists slack off. This is how costly and inefficient labor based economy was. It was very unproductive.

How the Economy Grows?

This chapter is about why the economy grows and why it crashes. For the first 1,800 years, the world did not have much economic growth. It is the past two centuries in which the world experienced an unprecedented level of prosperity. But what caused that to happen?

**Annualized Per Capita World GDP Growth
(Inflation Adjusted)**

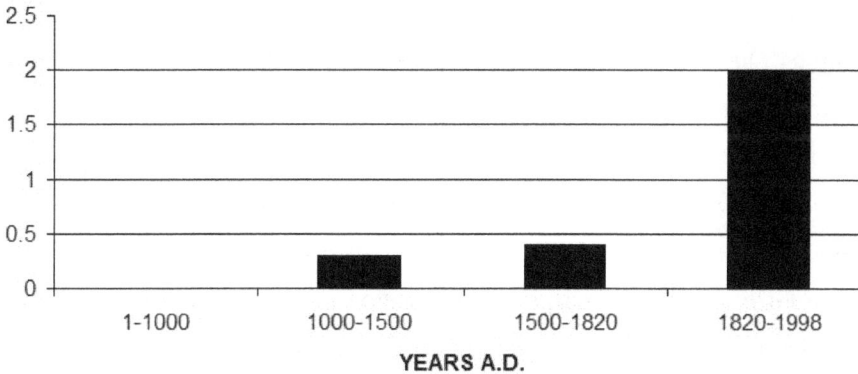

Source: Maddison, The World Economy: A Millennial Perspective , 264

Today, many experts think that economy grows by consumption. That's why government creates currency out of thin air and encourages spending. When the housing market or stock market corrects, the government supports it by bailing out companies or making the interest rate artificially low. By manipulating the market to show a healthy figure, they think our economy is growing. But does our economy grow this way? How does our economy grows? History had the answers.

The Rise of Great Britain

The 19th – 20th century marks the beginning or an era in the global economy – The *Industrial Revolution*. The revolution began in Britain when the economy evolved from a labor base towards a machine base manufacturing. Some of the major revolutionary changes include the use of refined coal, iron-making technique and textile industry. The born of the textile industry gave birth to the cotton industry.

One of the major shifts in human history is the invention of the steam engine. Steam engine soon became a power supply which surpassed waterfall and horsepower. It added a new chapter in the world energy history. Human moved from a lower energy concentration source to a higher energy concentration source. The applications of steam engines were enormous. One of them is railway. The first full scale working railway Steam locomotives first appear in UK in 1804. This dramatically reduced the time for people to travel from one place to another. The invention of the steam engine on railways also pushed the demand of coal and iron, as railway became an essential part of people's daily lives to transport of people and goods swiftly. This then sparked an expansion of the railway network to further improve economic growth. Later on, other nations began to copy the British railway model. By 1850 the British already had an well integrated railway transportation system which was on-time, fast and inexpensive. This stimulated a whole new level of business and job opportunities in the fields of electrical engineering, mechanical engineering, accountants, and railway employment etc. The increase of machinery and factories meant that Britain had an unprecedented advantage over mass produced low cost and high quality manufactured products. Britain committed itself wholly to a free trade policy, with few trade barriers on tariffs. From 1815 to 1870, she was renowned as *"The Workshop of the World"*. Do you see any similarities to China today? This is only phase one of the *Industrial Revolution*.

Phase two of the *Industrial Revolution* was more to do with inventions and technologies. Many streams of study in university today such as physics, medicine, engineering matured during the second phase of the industrial revolution. *Michael Faraday*, discovered the theory of electromagnetic induction in the mid 19th century, his invention of rotor device laid the foundation of electric motor technology. Around the same time, *Sir Joseph Swan*, developed the world first incandescent electric lamp which illuminates the world. Telegraph lines were installed along rail lines for communication with trains, and later on evolved into communication networks connecting cities around the world. The inexpensive process of mass producing steel further enhanced everything from infrastructure, building, ships, railway and other appliances. All these factors moved the world to the level of prosperity never experienced in the history of the world.

The standard of living improved dramatically. Price of goods fell because of the increase in productivity and efficiency. In Britain, goods were sold more cheaply in comparison with the rest of the world, although wages were still high. You see, technologies and inventions drives price down. This is the work of free market capitalism. There were little government interventions during the industrial revolution.

Lesson 15:

An economy grows by production. Technologies and Inventions drive prices down. Wages can be high while businesses can still make a profit under free market capitalism.

Just when everyone thought that British dominance was unquestionable, British reached the peak of her prosperity and began a downfall. But what caused this downturn? The British had a sound currency system, it was the *world factory* with both high productivity and technology. What was the tipping point of this prosperity? The answer laid in the pace of economic growth relative to the money supply.

The Fall of Great Britain

During the *Industrial Revolution*, Britain was not the only country who benefited. In fact, Britain faced many rivals in industrialization. The U.S. experienced the largest economic growth in the last two decades of

Industrial Revolution. Germany became the European primary industrial nation during that period. Overdevelopment was one of the reasons for the downturn. The British economy grew too fast, and people began to speculate. For example, the British had a bubble called *Railway Mania* in 1840. The railway was a very new way of transportating people during that period. People were over optimistic about the Railway system. Huge amounts of money were speculated in railway companies, which ultimately pushed the share price up. Many middle class families put their entire savings into railway companies during mania. When the bubble burst, they lost everything. The railway bubble was very much like the dot com bubble in 2000 except railway was something tangible.

The Long Depression (1873-1879) was probably the first global economic recession. Over speculation and optimism during the boom drove stock markets higher than the real economic growth. This lasted until the boiling point was reached. Countries which had overextended themselves suffered. Economy contracted. Railway was one of the sectors that was affected the most. Global output of iron and steel was down by 45%. Construction was down by 10%. Countries around the world experienced lower growth.

On the monetary side, the world economy was growing faster than the money supply. There was not enough Gold to back paid industrialization. In other words, there are too many goods relative to money. Price of goods needed to come down. This is *deflation* and is the exact opposite to what is happening today.

Lesson 16:

The Industrial Revolution caused economic growth. But speculation and over-optimism drove the stock markets overvalued relative to the real economic growth. Markets corrected inevitably. During the Industrial

Revolution, there were simply too many goods produced relative to the money supply. Price of goods needed to come down until business made a profit again. This is how the Free Market corrects itself during a contraction. This is deflation.

After the *Long Depression*, many people blamed the causes of falling prices was the root of all evil. People inherited the idea that economic contraction is always bad. It is not. Few noticed this is how the market rebalances itself. Here was what the famous economist Murry N. Rothbard explained.

"Unfortunately, most historians and economists are conditioned to believe that steadily and sharply falling prices must result in depression: hence their amazement at the obvious prosperity and economic growth during this era. For they have overlooked the fact that in the natural course of events, when the government and the banking system do not increase the money supply very rapidly, free market capitalism will result in an increase in production and economic growth so great as to swamp the increase in money supply. Price will fall, and the consequence will not be depression or stagnation, but prosperity (since costs are falling too) economic growth, and the spread of the increased living standard to all the customers."

Murray N. Rothbard was right. The global economy turned out much stronger after the *Long Depression*. However, the world learnt the wrong lesson which set the stage for the *Corruption of Real Money*.

The Actual Cause of the British's Fall

The Long Depression was not the cause of the British downfall. Sure it was weakened as rivals rose. But if it was not the depression, what caused it? Britain's true downfall began in 1914, a year after the Federal Reserve was created. If you studied world history, you might already have guessed what happened in the world that year. Yes... It was World War I.

WWI costed Britain its financial fortune. During WWI, Britain borrowed a large amount of money to fund the war. There was no limit to spending during the war. The objective of war is to destroy the enemy at all cost. Britain went from being the world's wealthiest creditor nation to the world's greatest debtor nation. The interest repayment alone was 40% of the government spending. Inflation was more than double between 1914 to 1920. Ultimately Britain was forced to move off the Gold Standard to finance the war. The British pound was devalued 61% during WWI, because as everyone was at war, the unemployment was very low.

After the war, soldiers returned home. Everything returned back to normal - all except one thing... The cost of living had become more expensive. In order to bring the cost down to the pre-war period, Britain knew it was necessary to return to Gold Standard, and they did it. But the worse was yet to come. By 1930, the "World" slided into *The Great Depression*. This put the final nail into the coffin of the British economy. Demand for British goods fell sharply. Unemployment skyrocketed to 20%. Foreigners who held British pounds wanted to exchange for gold. Gold was flown out to other countries, and the British money supply contracted. In September 1931, the British went off the Gold Standard once again. This marked the start of the decline of Great Britain.

Profits of War

War is expensive to fight but highly profitable to sponsor. What does that mean? How does sponsoring war become profitable? From history, we already knew all wars are financially destructive. Athens and Rome were a few of the examples demonstrating this fact. Fighting a war requires a country to perform deficit spending, and the result is the collapse of the economy.

But what makes war profitable? Under the Gold Standard, it is not economical to go to war. If a country is engaged in war, they need to export gold to import war equipment. If a country did not have enough gold, they needed to borrow from other nations in the form of War Bonds. Like Treasury Bonds, these were sold in the Open Market Operation. Because there were no limits to the demand for the war equipment needed. There were no limits to how much a country borrows to finance the war.

If you remember the birth of the Federal Reserve in 1913, it was created to provide an elastic currency supply and to act as a lender of the last resort after the lesson from *The Panic of 1907* banking crisis. It can create currency out of thin air by buying bonds directly from the Treasury. If we have a second look at the Federal Reserve, you will notice that WWI started only one year after the birth of the Fed. Could this be a coincidence? I suspected there were more functions to the creation of the Fed. I suspected it was used to fund wars. Unlike under the gold standard, where there is a fixed amount of wealth a country can fund the borrower, there are no limits to how much currency the Fed can create.

The transition of Britain's wealth to the U.S. began at the beginning of WWI. During WWI, Britain and France had to borrow heavily from the U.S. There were two powerful families acting as the sales agents of war bonds and war materials. They were the *Morgan* family from Britain and the *Rothschild* family from Europe. In other words, they had the role of being a middleman for the Allied and Axis forces. If you were the *Morgan* and *Rothschild*, would you want the war to end? Of course not. Under such an arrangement, you wouldn't worry which side was winning. Quite the opposite, you never wanted the war to end. The longer the war lasted, the more expenditure would be needed. The more hostile the war, the more war bonds countries would need to be purchased.

The Rothschild Formula

In fact, Grandad's book *The Creature of the Jekyll Island* has the magic formula to profit from war. It is called the *Rothschild formula.*

1 Government has to meet the challenge of war. It is a self-survival. You either win or perish. All else is secondary. Government will try whatever it can to win the war even at the expense of its citizens prosperity and the solvency of Treasury.

2 To engage war, a government need unlimited capital. Debt is the solution. All that necessary is for the government to maintain or expand its appetite for more debt. The greater the threat, the more destructive the war, the greater need for debt.

3 War not only needs enemies, but an enemy with credible military might. If such enemies already exist, all the better. If they exist but lack the military strength, fund them. If such an enemy does not exist, create one by financing the rise of a hostile regime.

4 If a government declines to finance its war through debt. Although it seldom happens, we need to overthrown the existing one with a government more compliant to our will. Assassination may be necessary in the process.

5 No nation is allowed to be militarily stronger than another. It will only lead to peace and a reduction of debt. A balance of power is needed. To accomplish this, we need to finance both side of the military conflicts. Unless one side is hostile to our interests, it must be destroyed. Otherwise neither side should be allowed a decisive victory or defeat. We must always proclaim the virtues of peace, the unspoken objective is perpetual of war.

Sinking Lusitania

Do you know prior to the U.S. entry into WWI, Germany almost won the war? At one stage, dark clouds were gathering at Wall Street as the war went bad for the Allied nations. Between 1914 and 1918, Germany submarines sunk over 5,700 surface ships. One out of four steamers left Britain and never returned. Germany was about to cut off Britain and her Allies from getting outside help. The morale of allied nations were very low indeed. Then, just as they were about to declare the loss of the war and made preparations to negotiate terms with Germany, a new event turned the war around.

The New York Times. EXTRA

LUSITANIA SUNK BY A SUBMARINE, PROBABLY 1,260 DEAD; TWICE TORPEDOED OFF IRISH COAST; SINKS IN 15 MINUTES; CAPT. TURNER SAVED, FROHMAN AND VANDERBILT MISSING; WASHINGTON BELIEVES THAT A GRAVE CRISIS IS AT HAND

Morgan had foreseen that if Germany won the war, he could no longer profit by selling war materials and war bonds to Allied nations, which meant his route to wealth would be cut off. Something needed to be done.

At that time, finance and banking were not Morgan's only business. He had steel, railway, ship building and propaganda etc. Sea transport was one of them. During the whole time, U.S played a neutral role in the war.

Since British no longer have the military might to compete with Germany, she needed to involve U.S. But how could Morgan convince U.S. to participate? How could he push U.S. off her stubborn neutrality?

A spark for war was needed. They needed a reason for U.S. to cry for war. They needed Germany to attack U.S. The plan Morgan used was unpatriotic, corrupted and cruel. On 7th May 1915, a U.S. ships, *Lusitania* carrying U.S. and British passengers was purposely lurked into military area of Germany. It was used as a bait to ignite sparks for military conflicts. It was sunk by Germany, approximately 1,260 were dead, and 195 were American. This is the Art of Rothschild Formula, sending civilians of his country to death on purpose. Soon Morgan used his power in propaganda and put fire into public sentiment in U.S., Their final goal was to sell the war to the American people. Words were spread by media through newspaper. Morgan was using the public pressure to force the U.S. government to enter the war. Germany was declared as the enemy of the western civilization.

Waves of angers pushed U.S to enter WWI. Within days of declaration, Congress voted $1 billion in credit for England and France, $200 Million was sent to England immediately deposited in Morgan's account. These were financed by the Fed and later on taxed the U.S citizens through inflation. Apart from the huge sum of money Morgan long waited, they made even more money through war equipment productions.

So you as a bright reader see that Morgan was using the Federal Reserve System to fund the war in the name of peace. They created currency to British and France and enslaved them in debt.

500 Million dollar loan contracted in autumn 1915 brought Morgan a net profit of 9 million dollars. By 1917, the French Government paid Morgan and other banks a commission of 1,500,000 dollar and further million in 1918....

Besides the loan, there was another source of profit: the purchase an sales of American stock which the Allies surrendered so that they could but munitions in the States. It is estimated that in the course of war, some 2000 million passed in this way through Morgan's hand. Even if commission was very small, transaction of such dimension would give him an influence on the stock market which would carry a very real advantage.....

His hatred against war did not prevent him, citizen of a neutral country, from furnishing belligerent power with 4,400,000 rifles for a matter of $194,000,000.... The profits were such as to compensate to some degree of his hatred on welfare. According to his own account, he received, as an agent of English and French governments, a commission of 1% on orders totaling $3,000,000,000.....

Source: Lewinsohn pp 103-4,222-24

"Nobody hates war more than I do." J.P. Morgan once said in public. Do you believe that? I leave the answer up to you.

What Happened to the Monetary System?

During the outbreak of WWI, Allies nations were exporting gold to purchase war equipments manufactured in U.S. Gold flowed into U.S as it became the world largest holder of Gold. When Allies nations no longer paid in gold, they indebted themselves by borrowing heavily from the U.S. With the sinking of the *Lusitania*, U.S entered the war. Like her Allies, the war expenditures were more than the income. With an ace held at hand, she operated the Federal Reserve to fund the war. From 1916 to May 1919, U.S national debt went from $1 billion to $25 billion. This marked a record of wartime fiscal deficit. The world money supply exploded.

Many would have guessed the inflation during the war would be astronomical. This was not the case. Quite the opposite, inflation during the U.S. wartime was slowing down rather than speeding up compared with the neutrality period (1914-1917) and the postwar 1918. With so much currency created during the inflation, it was thought that the wholesale prices would go higher. The reason is not the subject of this book. But I can give a brief explanation. Imagine if you have $1 million, during wartime you don't want to put so much money in the bank because of uncertainties. You hold $800,000 in cash and kept the remaining $200,000 at the bank. In order words, during wartime, you demand more currency, which is deflationary. The bank reserve will be low. Oppositely, after the war, people are quite comfortable to keep most of their currency in the bank. So there are less demand of currency. The bank will have more reserve.

Hang on a second. But wasn't the Fed funding the war by printing currencies? So how could we have less inflation? Yes, but if the currency drained by the public offset the expansion of the currency supply. The net result slowed down the inflation.

Rise of U.S.

After WWI, the U.S. held almost half of the world's gold inventory. Most European countries depleted their Gold and were indebted to the U.S. in dollars. The financial system using the classical Gold Standard no longer functioned properly. Since most of the world currency is in pounds and dollars, the dollar become more important as it began to share the world reserve currency status with British pounds. Only the pounds and U.S. dollar were redeemable in gold.

The Roaring 20s

It was a time of dawn. WWI was over. Fashion took a liberal turn. Jazz filled the airway. Charles Lindbergh caught the world's imagination with his flight from New York to Paris. Just about anyone who could afford to go to the movies. It was the *Roaring Twenties – The Jazz Age*.

My Grandad was born during the Roaring Twenties. During the 20s, the world had a vigorous expansion. The boom was partially fuelled by productivity and construction boom to rebuilt cities after war. New technologies changed everyone lifestyle. For the first time in history, it was possible for U.S. citizens to use credit to buy the product before they even had the money. *Buy now pays later* became a reality. People were not required to pay the full amount but only upfront. Six out of ten cars were purchased using credit. New products were developed that people didn't even know they need it prior to their invention. Customer goods like cars, refrigerators, and radio became a must have item. High tariff were implemented to protect local U.S manufacture industries. The stock market reflected that everyone is optimistic about the future. Dow Jones Industrial Average (DJIA) rose from 60 to 400 during 1921 to 1929. Soon Wall Street became the ticket to easy street for everyone. People mortgaged their home recklessly, invested their life saving in the stock market. Some people did end up becoming millionaires. Media reported that the stock market could never falls. Even though, there were two mild recessions to slow down the bull market, they appeared insignificant. The prosperity of the *Roaring Twenties* planted a perception on people that they were living in a fairy tale of a new era.

The Great Depression

At the peak of prosperity, very few people felt that a dark cloud was looming. The Great Depression of the 1930 was the most severe economic contraction in world financial history. The worldwide economic depression affected everyone, from young from to old, and from rich to poor. Even today, people use *The Great Depression* as a benchmark to understand how deep stock markets can fall. It all happened on 29 October 1929 when Wall Street stock market plummeted. That day was commonly known as *The Black Tuesday*.

During *The Great Depression*, many banks closed their door. People who deposited money in bank lost all their life savings. The entire banking system was on the brink of collapse. One out of every four people was unemployed. Price and production were cut down by one-third from the 1929 level. International trades collapsed. Australia, which relied heavily on export, was severely damaged. Falling prices put a downward pressure on wages. China suffered from overproduction of agricultural goods, depression caused the price to decline sharply. The effects on Great Britain were devastating. If you recall Britain was an industrialized nation, when demand for traditional industrial goods collapsed, many business needed to shut down. Unemployment doubled from 1 million to 2 million. Weimar Germany Republic was hit hard as well. After WWI, Germany signed the *Treaty of Versailles* to repay the damage they had done during the war. Massive war spending caused Germany to suffer hyperinflation. Various political and social tensions, which later on, shifted the power from the government to Hitler and his Nazi forces and triggered WWII. Germany unemployment was 30% during The Great Depression. Back in the U.S., the government tried to reverse *The Great Depression* by starting many government programs to create jobs. All of them declared failures at the end. On June 1930, U.S government implemented tariff on imports to encourage U.S citizen to buy U.S. made product. In retaliation, other nations did the same to raise tariff to U.S. made product, the depression only got worse.

Source: Elliott Wave International , 1999

So what caused *The Great Depression*? What was the trigger? Why was it so devastating? Why didn't the Federal Reserve stepped in as the white knight to save the economy? The lessons of 1930 were good lessons for us to project what will happen onwards from our economy. The things we are seeing today in our economy are **very similar** to what happened prior to *The Great Depression*. One of my primarily goal of *The Corruption of Real Money* is to race against time and alert as many people about this before it happens. We will face a similar crisis as early as this decade.

Even today, many people are puzzled by the cause of *The Great Depression*. They believe it was an act of God. But *The Great Depression* did not occur without a warning. There were a lot of indicators during the *Roaring 20s*. Before I to explain why, please understand I cannot outline all the factors in here as the subject of *The Great Depression* can be a book of its own. If you want to know more, I recommend you to read *Murray N Rothbard, American Great Depression* as it explains the subject in detail. If you look at the DJIA in the previous page, we know that the bigger the boom, the bigger the crash. If the economy overextends itself beyond reality by having too much credit or debt, a crash is inevitable. Now let's be a monetary detective and investigate what happened through the rubbles of *The Great Depression*.

Factor 1: Helping Britain

Unlike the U.S., Britain's economy was in grave danger during the *Roaring Twenties*. Unemployment was high. Prolonged wars and huge deficit spending damaged her economic structure. Britain had to go back to the Gold Standard to resolve the root of the problem. Pre-WWI, British pound sterling to U.S. dollar, was set at £1=$4.87 and gold was £4.24/oz. If Britain was to return to Gold Standard, gold would have cost more than £4.24/oz, say 20% increase to £5/oz to reflect war inflation. But the problem is that if Britain was to use the old exchange rate of £1=$4.87

to remain competitive in her backbone business on export, she would need to have a price decline by an equivalent 20% of goods sold. If this was the case, businesses would have to lower wages and cause further unemployment. This was definitely not a political option but ironically was the right option. Instead of allowing the contraction of credits, and the free market to determine the gold price. Britain inflated her money supply to offset the loss of gold. [Note: Each country must declare a fixed ratio between gold and their own currency. In US , 1 ounce of gold = $20.64 USD and in Britain, 1 ounce of gold =£4.24. This gives a relationship of £1=$4.87.]

The corruption of real money began in Britain as people started to become addicted to cheap credit. But how did the U.S. help Britain? The Federal Reserve governor, *Benjamin Strong,* opted to help Britain to continue their trade at the expense of inflating the U.S money supply. (e.g. printing money until one ounce of gold was worth more than it was to maintain £1=$4.87 exchange rate). By doing this, Britain would no longer need to lose gold to the U.S. Choosing inflation in the U.S. to help Britain was one of the steps contributing to *The Great Depression.*

Factor 2: Dollar and Gold Reserve

In the previous chapter, we define inflation as an increase in the currency supply. This is not very precise under the Gold Standard. Inflation should be defined as the increase in total currency supply not covered by an increase in gold. The more dollar covered by gold, the sounder would our currencies be, because the more value a dollar could maintain. You see from the table below, between June 1921 and June 1929, the total dollar claimed rose faster than the gold reserve. Total dollar uncovered rose from $42.1 to $68.8 billion. Cheap credit was corrupting real money. This was another catalyst triggering *The Great Depression.*

Total Dollars and Total Gold Reserves:
(billions of dollars)

Uncovered Dollars	Total Dollar Claims	Total Gold Reserve	Total
June, 1921	44.7	2.6	42.1
June, 1929	71.8	3.0	68.8

Source: American Great Depression, Murray N. Rothbard pg 94

Factor 3: Demand Deposit to Time Deposit

Another good reason worth investigating is that depositors shift from demand deposit to time deposit. We already knew that time deposit allows the banks to keep a lower reserve. Depositors choose time deposit to get a better rate of return. Between June 1921 to June 1929, we saw a significant shift from demand deposit to time deposit. The demand deposit increased 30.8% but the time deposit increase more than 70%!

Total Dollars and Total Gold Reserves:
(billions of dollars)

%Demand Deposit	Demand Deposit	Time Deposit	Total
June, 1921	17.5	16.6	51.3
June, 1929	22.9	28.6	44.5

Source: American Great Depression, Murray N. Rothbard pg 99

The increase in time deposit was not accidental. Before the Federal Reserve was created, it was not legitimate to pay interest on time deposit, it was the Federal Reserve Act which pass this law and later on became one of the inflation catalyst.

Failure of New Deal

Despite President *Roosevelt*'s efforts to rearrange the economy and interfere with the free markets through various government programs called *New Deal*, the Great Depression resurfaced in 1937. In the U.S., production and profit declined sharply. Unemployment was as high as it was back in 1932. The combined states and federal expenditure on welfare rose from virtually nothing ($9 million) to $479 million from 1930 to 1940. An additional $480 million was spent on unemployment benefits. This caused a lot of inflation in the currency supply. All these currencies spent cannot resolved *The Great Depression*, and the worst of all, people became increasingly reliant on the government and cheap credits. The Fed became more powerful as more and more people became dependent on it.

Wrong Lessons Learnt from Big Mistakes

The *New Deal* did not cure *The Great Depression*. *New Deal* was a government intervention scheme tried to pop up the deflating bubble by expanding the money supply. If the free market were allowed to work, and the bubble were allowed to be fully deflated, the economy would cleanse its toxic and once again return to its healthy state. But there was one problem. For the bubble of that magnitude to deflate completely, the global economic must go through a painful and dreadful period. Unfortunately, the mass did not understand this. It was politically unpopular. People were complaining that the Federal Reserve policy were so supine. That's why Ben Bernanke famously said

> *"Deflation : Make sure "It" Doesn't happen here"*
> **Ben Bernanke, Chairman of the Federal Reserve, 2001**

Even today, there are endless debates by different schools of economics as to whether the Federal Reserve should have done something, *The Great Depression* would have been better. In reality, there would be no difference. The Fed's policy will be just like Roosevelt's *New Deal*, it could only treat the symptom rather than cure the disease. Ironically, many economists today still learnt the wrong lessons. Even so, in reality, the Great Depression did not end completely by natural recovery nor the Federal Reserve monetary policies. It was ended by one of the biggest world events in the 20th century.

The World War II Medicine

Just when everyone was about to lose hope in the U.S., news came that World War II had begun. WWII was the deadliest war recorded in the 20th Century. Death ranged from 50 million to 70 million people. It all started in Weimar Germany because political pressure of *Treaty of Versailles* and *The Great Depression* damaged the German economy severely. The German middle classes simply had no way out. They felt betrayed by the government. They needed someone with visions to lead them. This eventually led to the rise of *Adolf Hitler* and the *Nazi Party*. They overthrew the government by offering people a way out. They sought vengeance from Britain by first invading Poland. WWII officially started in 1939.

Poland never will rise again in the form of the Versailles treaty. This is guaranteed not only by Germany, but also…Russia.

-Adolf Hitler, public speech in Danzig at the end of September 1939

Back in U.S, just as unemployment continued to plague the country again, WWII quickly turned the tide. Back then, the U.S agreed to supply Britain, Soviet Union, China, France and allied nations with a total of $50.1 billion worth of war equipments to meet the demand. U.S. manufacturing industries once again stepped on the accelerator. It went from high unemployment to full employment. Women also actively participated in war manufacturing jobs which were previously considered only men's work. New industries previously non-existent prior to the war, were developed. A whole new array of guns, ships, battle cruisers, planes and tanks were built. Overall productivity soared.

During WWII, government spenting was unprecedented. Between 1940 to 1945, Federal Spending went from $9.47 billion to $72.11 billion. Military spending went from $1.66 billion to $64.53 billion. These might not sound a lot in today's dollar terms, but it was an astronomically large number during that period. The government also advertised for people to buy war bonds, these were similar to loans but from the government. Government promised to pay back interests on those bonds after 10 years or more. Apart from that, people paid high taxes. Even Disneyland cartoons like Donald Duck and Bugs Bunny put a lot of effort on WWII propaganda. They encouraged Allies to work together to fund the war against Axis.

At the end, Allies declared a victory. Although there was massive government spending and high taxes, what the government did with that money was invest in building factories, in infrastructures and built military goods for unlimited demand by Allies. So the government made good use of the currencies they created and taxed. This enormous amount of capital return successfully, and lifted the U.S. out of *The Great Depression.*

Lesson 17:
Even though a lot of currencies were created in WWII, the government made good use of their capitals by investing in manufacturing and production. They were not using the printed money on consumption like today. Massive productions during WWII exceeded the money supply, which eventually drove the world out of The Great Depression.

After WWII, many people feared the world would slide back into *The Great Depression*, but it did not. Miracles happened. World economies prospered to a greater extend during the post war life. But after WWII, shouldn't there be significantly less demand for military goods, so what had happened?

During the post war period, automobile industries converted back into producing cars, new industries like aviation and electronic boomed. When soldiers retuned back home, there was a housing boom, which was successfully stimulated by affordable mortgages. National GDP jumped from $200,000 million in 1940 to $300,000 in 1950, and then to $500,000 in 1960. *Baby Boomers* were born. Eventually, the U.S. became the greatest creditor nation in the world. In fact it had more foreign assets than all other creditors nations in the world combined.

Evolution of the Financial System

On July 1944, 44 Allied nations gathered at the Mount Washington Hotel in Bretton Woods, New Hampshire for a conference. The purpose was to set up a system of rules, and procedures to regulate the international financial system after WWII. It is referred to today as *The Bretton Wood System.* Two international agencies were created at the conference. They were the *International Monetary Fund (IMF)* and its sister organization, *Bank for Reconstruction and Development*, which later on known as *World Bank.*

World Bank was designed to make loans to developing countries to help them build up a stronger economy. IMF was to promote monetary corporation between nations by maintaining a fixed exchange rate between countries.

After the war, the entire international financial system was devastated. There was a huge imbalance in the quantity of currency between countries. Because most of the international trades were based on borrowing from U.S., so she was the biggest creditor nation. During that time, many countries around the world were holding U.S. dollars, and the U.S. was the biggest gold holder in the world, so the U.S. dollar was agreed to be used as the world reserve currency backed by gold fixed at \$35/oz. Since then, the U.S. dollar was as good as gold.

To understand the evolution of the financial system we have to go all the way back to the 17th century. Are you ready?

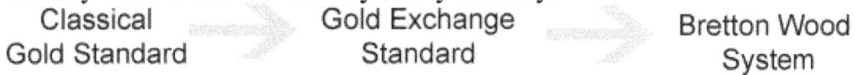

| Classical Gold Standard | → | Gold Exchange Standard | → | Bretton Wood System |

Classical Gold Standard (1815 – 1914)

Amount of Gold control the amount of paper currency produced

Under the *Classical Gold Standard*, the amount of currencies issued were based on how much gold a country produced. This made the money supply very stable. Because only a certain quantity of gold will be minted each year, the increase in money supply was predictable. Loosely speaking, the entire world money supply was all the weight of the gold ever mined. Back then, currencies (e.g. banknotes) were claim checks for the gold(i.e. money). That's why J.P. Morgan said gold is money, nothing else.

Gold Exchange Standard (1926 – 1931)

During WWI, many governments around the world indebted themselves by devaluing their currency to fund the war. Under the *Classical Gold Standard*, there will not be enough gold to cover all the currency that was created. So that's why there was a need to redefine the price of gold. This applies to all currencies like the *franc, mark, pound, dollar* etc. Under the classical gold standard, a unit weight of gold was $20.64 USD or £4.24. Britain was under grave economic problem. A lot of Gold was outflow. She faced a difficult choice between saving her export industry or worsening unemployment. Going back to classical gold standard was impossible. They seek U.S. for help.

After WWI, U.S. was the largest holder of gold in the world. A lot of U.S. dollars were held outside the U.S. by Allies nations. To help Britain, U.S chosen to inflate their own currency supply to maintain a healthy exchange rate for Britain's export. Since Britain pound was the world reserve currency, and U.S. dollar was pegged to most of the Gold. Thus, this formed a relation like below. This was the gold exchange standard.

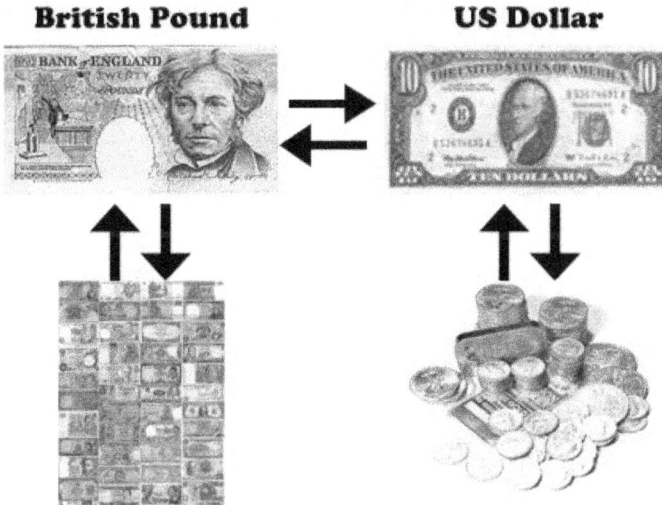

British Pound   **US Dollar**

In the end, Britain never really went back to the Classical Gold Standard. It chose to use cheap credit with the help of the U.S to keep the economy stable. The Gold exchange standard was a man-made system. It relied on the U.S. and Britain's central bank monetary policies to keep the exchange rate stable. It was not a self adjustment mechanism like the Classical Gold Standard.

Bretton Woods System (1944 – 1971)

After WWII, the U.S evolved to become the largest creditor in the world and held $26 million in gold reserve, which was approximately 60% of the world's gold. It was also the biggest lender in the world, many of the countries were holding U.S. dollar denominated securities. Because the gold exchange standard was incapable to cope with world trade, 44 Allied nations gathered together in *Bretton Woods* to agree a new monetary system. The conclusion was that all currencies were redeemable in U.S dollars, which was pegged to gold at $35/oz. This marked an important point in monetary history. The U.S. dollar was as good as gold. What *Bretton Woods* system really meant was that all world currencies had to exchange for U.S. dollar before they could claim Gold. Ever since, the world became dependent on the U.S. dollar.

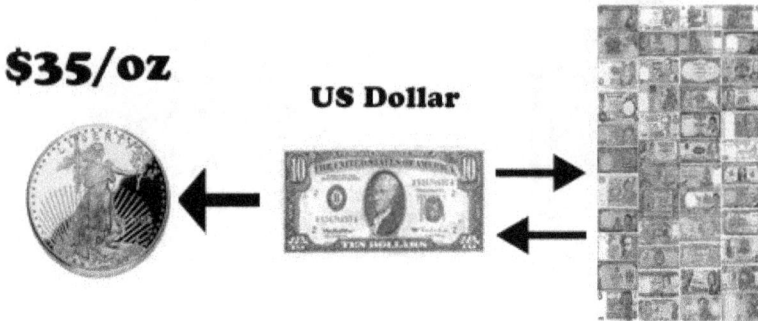

$35/oz

US Dollar

Nixon Shock

It appeared that U.S. economy was invincible, just like the early Britain. No one would ever have guessed her economy began to fall at the peak of prosperity. While enjoying the prosperity from its founding fathers, the U.S. government started to become creative. They wanted to dominate the world in the name of being the world police. They chose to invest in military spending rather than production. U.S. President Lyndon Johnson's Guns and Butter Administration was an example. The country was led to fight Vietnam war. They compete with U.S.S.R in the space program by sending men to the moon at the expense of it unshakable financial position after WWII.

With the huge deficit spending in the 60s, U.S. was on the brink of losing her financial fortune. She needed to find a way to keep her gold at all cost. On August 15, 1971, U.S. President Nixon convinced the entire world to replace gold with U.S. Dollar by closing the gold window. Gold standard was obsolete. Since then, all the world currencies became fiat simultaneously. The reason why we see so much volatility today, like oil price going up 10 times, real estate going up 10 times, gold going from $35/oz to $1700/oz is because of Nixon's decision.

In the absence of Gold Standard, there is no real adjustment mechanism to keep trade imbalance in check. With the U.S. dollar remains as the world reserve currency, and the Federal Reserve ability to expand and contract the currency supply, U.S. has the privilege to print unlimited amount of U.S dollar to exchange for all the goods and services produced by the rest of the world. The corruption of real money had begun.

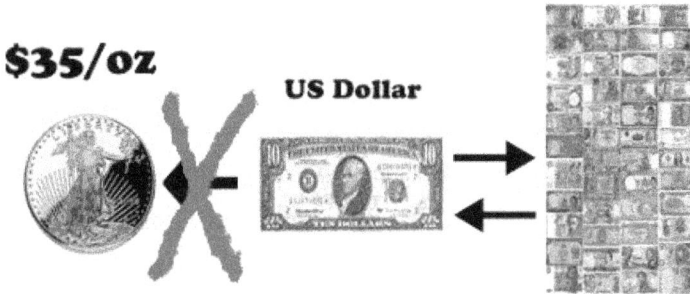

$35/oz   **US Dollar**

1971 Nixon Close the Gold Window

The Rules of the Game Had Changed

Under the *Bretton Woods* System, when one country exported more than it imported to the U.S., that country would be in trade surplus. The U.S would need to export gold in return for the goods and services she received. Under such an arrangement, the U.S monetary supply would contract until it reached a point where it would be trade competitive again.

When the gold window was closed, the world was under the Dollar Standard. Things played out very differently. Take China and the U.S. trade relationship as an example, China was the largest holder of foreign exchange reserve of approximately $3 trillion USD in 2011. What that's means was that China sold $3 trillion worth of goods more than U.S sold to her. This imbalance in trade would have been impossible under the gold standard. The reason why China is still holding that much U.S denominated assets today is because everyone in the world still has the perception that USD has value. This was true when the USD was pegged to gold, but it is no longer true as the values of the USD and other currencies are entirely based on people perception that we are all dreaming the same dream!

Lesson 18:

What we are experiencing today is a direct result of what happened in the past. In the absence of the gold standard for benchmarking, countries become addicted to using cheap credit to grow their economy. Government forgets that an economy grows by production, innovation and saving. They encourage people to borrow and consume in order to grow the economy, to continue our prosperity or to fight off recession. Growth should not be based on debts, as the more debts we use, the more inflation we will have. This generation or the next will eventually pay the price.

The world monetary system evolved from a classical gold standard to gold exchange standard, and then to Bretton Woods system, and now to The Dollar Standard. Under the Dollar standard, all the world currencies became fiat simultaneously. Today, the values of our currencies are not derived from gold which has intrinsic value, they are derived from our perception, our faith and government mandates.

In the next chapter, we will enter the realm of where we are today-The age of paper currency.

Chapter 8

How to Predict a Financial Crisis?

"There is no means of avoiding the final collapse of a boom brought about by credit expansion. The alternative is only whether the crisis should come sooner as the result of voluntary abandonment of further credit expansion, or later as a final catastrophe of the currency system involved."

–Ludwig Von Mises

"Prior to natural disasters, you may have heard tales about pets and livestock acted strangely. Dogs barked non-stopped. Wildlife fled in groups. Earthworm poured out from the ground. Animal indeed had a sixth sense to natural disasters. Most people do not." Grandad explained.

An Unfair Advantage

"Why can't people see disasters coming?" I said curiously.

"Ignorance. This is true for both natural and financial disasters. Most people, even the government, believed they can outsmart the market force. When the financial crisis became out of their control, they were just reactionary to what had already happened. Eventually fear drove the market."

"But the government eventually stabilized the market, right?"

"On the surface, they did. The market did return to normal. However if you look beneath the surface, most government solutions were merely

153

short term fix for a long term pain. The fundamental problems were not resolved."

"Huh? So will the crisis resurface someday?"

"I am sure it will. But it will probably be after my times. It will be your generation's problem." Grandad smiled.

"That's.........unfair..." I murmured.

"Unfair?" Grandad chuckled.

"Grandad, don't you think it is unfair and irresponsible?" I protested. I felt anger as our generation is going to face problems passed on by the baby boomers era.

"To people who choose to ignorance, it will be unfair, but to those who understand the root of the problem it can be an unfair advantage."

"An unfair advantage?"

"Remember that there are always two sides to every coin. Other people's problems maybe your opportunities. Now you have some knowledge about world monetary history. It is time to learn something new. But I have to warn you first, it is going to be difficult. "

"Please Grandad, I really want to learn. Please tell me." I insisted as I jumped up and down.

"Once you learnt this knowledge it will become your little crystal ball. The financial system painted by the media and the government is not the actual picture, there is another picture behind it. The stuff you are hearing on television or the media are just smoke screens to cover the flaws of the financial world. By understanding the fundamental concepts about how markets behave is like you are removing the fog so that you can plan ahead of what will happen. Now, Ching, are you ready to built your crystal ball?"

"I am ready!"

Where are we today?

Since the breakdown of the Bretton Woods system in 1971, we were all living in a Dollar Standard. All world currencies were pegged to U.S dollar backed by nothing but faith of the U.S. government. The self adjustment mechanism of gold keeping the trade deficit in check disappeared. U.S. did not need to pay gold in return for goods and services imported. Instead, she paid IOUs. Since, 1949, the gold reserve had been declining from 70% down to less than 5%. Foreign exchange reserve (i.e. other assets backed by currency) increased from 30% to 90%. Real money was corrupted. New generations are brainwashed to believe fiat currency is money. This opened the Pandora box of the corruption of real money.

Why the World Prospers after it Unpegs from Gold

"Grandad, if the gold standard was so good, why would unpegging the dollar from gold creates an unprecedented level of prosperity?" I was right. Thirty years after the collapse of Bretton Woods system, the world enjoyed an unprecedented boom in history. U.S. was still the driver of economic growth, but instead of being the leading export of goods and service to the rest of the world, it became the leading export of IOUs. The world depended on exporting goods to the U.S in return for IOUs for growth. This model created a miracle for U.S. being able to import indefinitely far more than to export. In return for these IOUs, the credit market in the world expanded. That's why there are far more currencies created today than anytime in history. The credit expansion flown into the stock market and real estate market and caused asset price to rise. This gigantic boom happened as if we had discovered an enormous stockpile of gold. That's why when you talk to post-war baby boomers today, they have the perception that they are now living in a new era.

If you were in generation Y, your parent would urge you to broad the real estate train as early as possible. This plan worked well for them, but will it continues to work well for you? As I am writing now, I am afraid to say that we had passed our peak prosperity based on debt fuelled growth.

Why Predicting a Financial Crisis?

"Grandad, do you mean financial crisis can make you wealthy?"

"Absolutely" Grandad explained. "The road to true wealth is by understanding money and business cycles. Financial crisis is a representation of these business cycles."

"But how does that work? Most of the time it devastates people wealth!"

"Not really. Market goes up, and the market goes down. In a financial crisis, someone lost money to someone else. This is a pain and a gain. If there is no pain, then there will be no gain. It depends if you want to be the one suffer in pain or enjoy the gain."

How to Predict A Financial Crisis?

"But there are many factors and uncertainties affecting the market."

"Indeed. The short term fluctuations are difficult to catch. But the long term trend is there. Predicting a financial crisis is not magic, it is governed by sets of indicators with charts and numbers. Being able to read charts is like doctors being able to use X-rays screening for diagnosis. With your new skills of using financial X-rays, you too will be able to tell whether a financial crisis is coming, how severe if it hit, and how to profit from it. These indicators are not made up. They had triggered major financial crises in the past."

Imbalance of Payment

The first X-ray Grandad taught me was called the *Balance of Payment*. These concepts might be difficult to understand in the first time. So please feel free to go back and re-read them.

The *Balance of Payment* (BOP) measures all the economic transactions of the dollar and goods. Every international transaction is an exchange of money (i.e. currency) with value (i.e. goods and services). For example, if the U.S. imports milk from Australia, first it has to supply U.S dollar to exchange for Australian Dollar in order to import milk. So milk represents the value that is coming into U.S and U.S. dollar is the currency that is flowing out of the country. That is what happened when a country imports goods and services. Values come in, and currencies go out. The U.S. dollar is sold in the foreign exchange market in exchange for Australian dollar. How about if U.S is buying financial assets like the Australian government bonds instead of goods? The same thing happens. The U.S will need to sell U.S. dollar in the foreign exchange market to buy Australian dollar in order to purchase the bond. But what about export? Say, for example, if U.S is exporting rulers to China. The Chinese business owner has to exchange the Chinese *Renminbi* for the U.S dollar to pay for the rulers. So in this case currencies are flowing in the U.S, and values (i.e. rulers) are flowing out of the U.S. If you add up all these transactions together, the dollars flowing in and out have to balance somehow. This is what *Balance of Payment* is all about.

Without going too much into the technical aspect but retain a degree of accuracy, *Balance of Payment* composed of two accounts. The first one is called *Current Account*, and the second one is called *Capital and Financial Account*. The *Current Account* measures the trade of goods and services between countries and the *Capital and Financial Account* measure the flow of capital between countries. The *Balance of Payment* is summarized by the formula below.

Current account = Capital and Financial Account + Reserve Asset

Ideally, for *BOP* to be balanced, the *Current Account* must be equal to the *Capital and Financial Account*. The deficit on *Current Account* must be exactly offset by the surplus on *Capital and Financial Account*. However, it is never the case. This is where the *Reserve Asset* comes in play. The difference between these two accounts is made up by the *Reserve Asset*. These *Reserve Assets* can be gold, holding of foreign currencies, or *Special Drawing Right* (SDR which is IMF's special currencies). So a country's overall balance can be though of as a change in her *Reserve Asset*. Do you follow me so far?

But the problem is that there is a very big difference between Reserve Assets under Gold Standard and Reserve Asset today. Gold cannot be printed by the government. Unlike other financial assets, gold cannot be created magically to finance an imbalance of payment. In other words, under the gold standard, deficit countries were required to pay their deficit in gold (limited). Today, deficit countries may settle their deficits with debt (unlimited).

The original idea of accumulating *Reserve Assets* was like a saving for a rainy day, just like saving money in case of emergency needs. Ironically accumulating too much Reserve Asset is the core reason which leads to the *Great Japanese Bubble* in the 80s and the *Asian Financial Crisis* in 1997.

The Lost Decades of Japan

The first victim of the excessive accumulation excessive reserve is Japan. By the end of 1980, the land price of Japan had risen to a level that the land price of the Imperial Garden in Tokyo were said to be more than the State of California! The Nikkei index had an extraordinary surge from less than 5,000 in the early 70s to 38,000 by 1989. This is 7.6 times from its 1972 low.

Nikkei Index

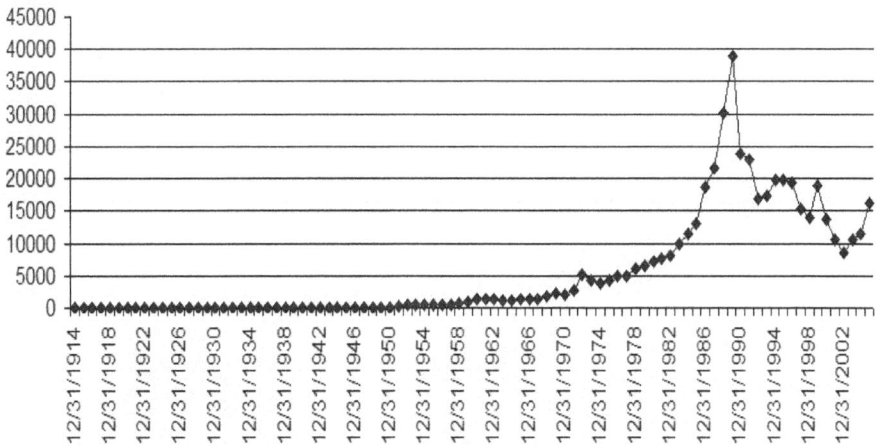

Source: http://www.finfacts.com/

If you lived through the 80s, you might have already heard that the economic growth of Japan was a miracle. 20 years after WWII, it came back as the world's second largest economy with economic growth averaging 10% in the 60s. Its export-led growth strategy was a huge success.

But how did Japan's economy downfall? Japan had a high saving rate. It did not have deficit spending. It manufactured and exported. It innovated and produced. Didn't we conclude that productivity and innovation led to prosperity? What triggered the lost decades of Japanese economy?

During the 80s, IMF only warned about the danger of trade deficits. There were not much mentioning about trade surplus. The huge trade surplus resulted in huge capital influx into Japanese Banking sector.

Through fractional reserve banking, this capital further multiplied many times. This caused the economy to overheat and rise of asset price.

To cool down the economic growth, one of the options the Japanese had was to issue bonds, or export capital (Capital account deficit), to absorb the excessive capital. If the capital account deficit is large enough to offset the current account surplus. Then the balance of payment will have little impact. The Reserve Assets will remain fractional.

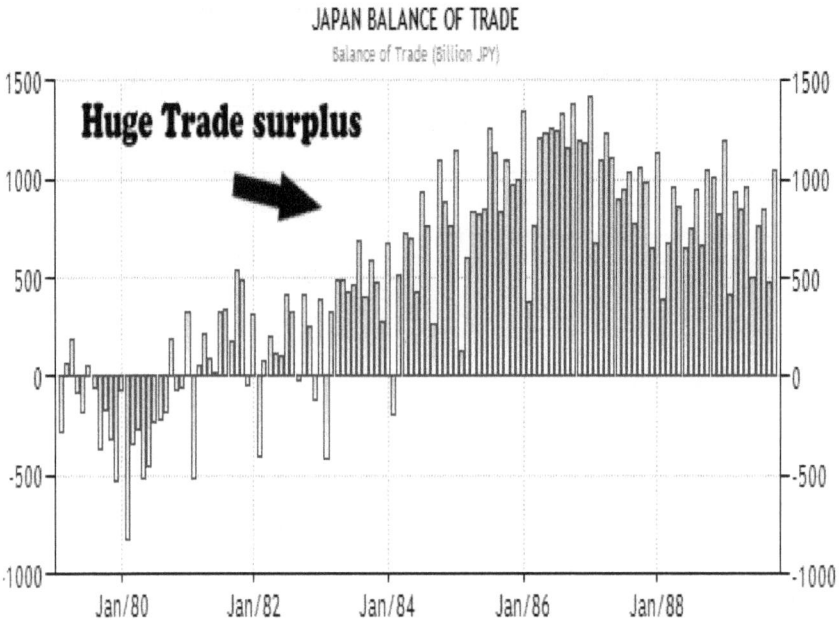

JAPAN BALANCE OF TRADE
Balance of Trade (Billion JPY)

Huge Trade surplus

Source: http://www.tradingeconomics.com/

[Note: If you recall how the Federal Reserve controls the money supply, buying bonds means expanding the currency supply; issuing bonds to public and pay back interests will draw capital from the public.]

In reality, the *Current Account* surplus was rising faster than the export of capital. Too much *Reserve Asset* caused asset price to inflate too fast.

Excessive capital allows businesses to overexpand and further increase the production. People over invested in companies and surged the stock and real estate market. At one point, rise in income cannot catch up with the rapid rise in asset price. Businesses defaulted on loans and stock market imploded. Price of goods and profits dropped rapidly as credit began to contract. The great Japanese Bubble ended in deflation which continues even as I am writing today.

Can Printing Money Cure Deflation?

To combat inflation, rising interest rate to tighten the money supply might be effective. However, when it comes to deflation, increasing the money supply will not help. You can fight fire with fire, but you cannot fight water with water. This was exactly what the Japanese government did from the advice of the Federal Reserve. That was why in the last chapter I emphasized a wrong lesson was learnt from *The Great Depression*. Most government thinks that any economic difficulties can be overcome by increasing or decreasing the money supply. This is a grave mistake. Peter Schiff of Euro Pacific Capital once gave a very good analogy to describe this. Suppose credit as the alcohol. Drinking alcohol will cause the economy to go high, everyone will be happy as long as our economy continues to grow. But drinking too much alcohol will cause the economy to get drunk and sick. To recover, our economy needs to detox through painful recessions. Giving more credit to a drunken economy is preventing the market to recover. Eventually, too much alcohol will kill the patient.

The Asian Financial Crisis

After the burst of the Great Japanese bubble, our policy makers, the government around the world, and the IMF seemed to learn very little from the origin of the crisis. No one seemed to have a sixth sense to what was coming. When the Asian Financial Crisis hit in 1997, no one knew what was going on.

"We have currency going down and down and down...we felt totally helpless and we feel tht there is no way we can recover..the feeling was really, really bad, really frightening."
-Dr Mahathir bin Mohamad- Prime Minister of Malaysia

"The Fund Manager did not know the difference between Indonesian, Thailand, Singapore, they just say I want out!Property price collapsed. Companies collapsed. As in the case of Indonesian, the social founding collapse..."
-Lee Kuan Yew – Senior Minister of Singapore

"It was unbelievable that the crisis had spread as quickly to Indonesian and Korea, within a matter of six months or seven months. It was much more globalize than we though"
–Eisuke – Minister of Finance of Japan, 1997-1999

Asian Financial Crisis was a crisis too mysterious to everyone when hit. It spread quickly like a contagion from one country to another, and another. Everyone panicked. Later on, almost everyone believed that the origin of the crisis was caused by a sudden outflow of capital from countries. That was what happened, but ironically it was not the causes. The causes can be found out from our financial X-Ray.

Source: Wikipedia

The origin of Asian Financial Crisis began in Thailand. Unlike Japan, Thailand financial crisis was not caused by a trade surplus (Current Account surplus). In fact, Thailand was running a huge trade deficit. If you lived through 80s and 90s, you might have heard that Thailand economy was booming, the market skyrocketed. Property price in Thailand rose over 1000%! Government needed to build more houses to push the price down. At one stage, there was so many constructions going on, people joked that the crane was Thailand's national bird. But how did Thailand's economic boomed so quickly while it was running a huge trade deficit? There must be a huge foreign capital inflow in Thailand to make that happen.

If you back trace the root of the crisis, the key to it was Japan. During the mid 80s, the appreciating Yen caused many Japanese companies to reallocate their manufacturing base to the rest of Asia. Thailand was one of them. An extraordinary amount of foreign capital inflow into Thailand economy created a tremendous boom. This boosted the *Capital and*

Financial Account of Thailand and offset its huge trade deficit (Current Account deficit).

Thailand Current Account Balance (1980 - 1996)

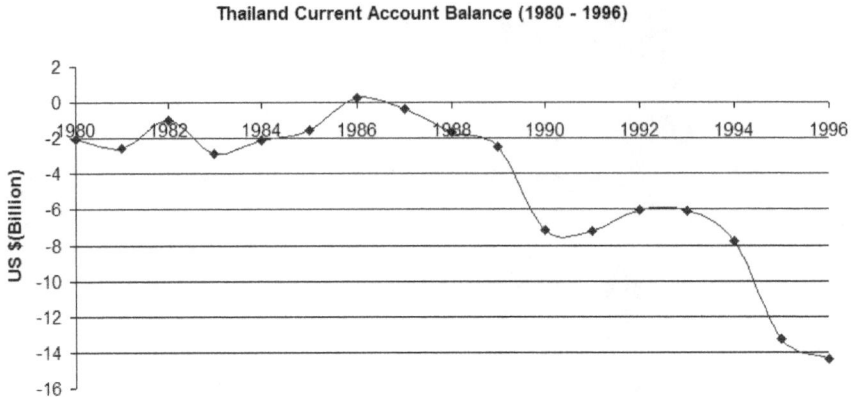

Source: http://www.indexmundi.com/thailand/current_account_balance.html

As you see from the last section, Japan had a huge Reserve Assets, and they needed to reinvest them in other countries to cool down their economy. So Japan's huge *Current Account* Surplus did not only create a credit bubble in Japan, but it also caused other economic bubbles later on in other Asian countries. If you followed me up to this point. You understood the big picture. Part of the reason of the existence of these huge Reserve Assets came from U.S. running huge trade deficit to the rest of the world through the Federal Reserve bond buying.

During that time, Thai companies found that they could raise large capital through the international bond market, and foreign banks want to lend money to Thailand because of the attractiveness of high interest rate, this fuelled huge capital inflow and short term "hot money" to enter the Thai economy. This foreign capital drove the stock market to unprecedented high level. Businesses increase their capacity and over expanded. Because there were large amount of cross border investments, Thailand was more exposed to exchange rate risks. During that time, most of these loans were denominated in U.S. dollar and have short maturity. When the dollar rose, and Thai Baht could not catch up fast enough with the appreciating dollar, then problems came. Since Thailand borrowed a considerable amount of capital from overseas lenders, when the Thai Baht's value falls sharply against U.S. dollar, the debt burden remains. With dollar denominated debt combines with the interest payment, it was costing Thailand more to repay the debt in terms of Baht. Eventually, businesses went bankrupts as they failed to meet their debt obligations. The stock market collapsed 95% of its nominal value in 1993 as foreign dumped Thai stocks. Thai Baht devalued 50% against the dollar. But even so, who would have imagined a small economy such as Thailand could spark a global financial crisis?

Before the crisis hit Malaysia, the country's economy was stable. The rate of inflation and unemployment were low. The economy was even growing at a rate of 8.7%. There were no observable weaknesses in the overall financial structure. So the financial crisis was not because of the economic foundation. The root of all evil was due to the accumulation of too much Reserve Asset! Between 1991 and 1993, Malaysia Reserve Asset doubled. Between 1990 and 1997, bank loans went from 5 billion to almost 25 billion Malaysian ringgit.

The same dynamic happened in Philippines, Singapore, Indonesia, Hong Kong, Korea and Taiwan. All Asian Tiger economies previously overdeveloped suffers the same consequence. At the end, many countries' currencies devalue against U.S dollar like Thailand with Hong Kong being an exception.

Lesson 19:

Excessive trade surplus or inflow of capital helps to build up huge Reserve Assets. Too much Reserve Assets overheat the economy. Since U.S became the world economic growth engine through debts, countries were relying on exporting to U.S to build up excessive reserves, which would have been impossible under the Gold Standard. Huge Reserve Asset overheats the economy and creates unsustainable asset bubbles, causing boom and burst cycles. Excessive foreign capital inflow overheats the economy and exposes it to exchange rate risk.

Where is the Center of Gravity of our Currency Supply?

If you can observe the center of gravity of our currency supply, you know which way the value of our currency is going to swing next. What does the centre of gravity of currency supply suppose to mean? It may sound abstract at the beginning but actually the concept is quite simple. Say, for example, under the Gold Standard, our currency supply expands with the mint of gold. For the sake of simplicity, if half of the currency issued were back by gold at $100/oz and the other half is backed at $200/oz. The fair market value of money will be roughly around $150/oz. This is the center of gravity of our currency supply. Even so, the center of gravity of money cannot be concluded over a short period. It needs to be observed over a very long timeframe (e.g. a minimum of five years or even decades) to be accurate.

But what does this center of gravity of money suppose to tell us? If the price of our currency is higher than this center of gravity, it means there are more currencies created relative to gold. Then the economy will show deflationary effects to revert to the equilibrium. Likewise, if the price of our currency is lower than this center of gravity, the economy will show inflationary effects. Either case, the currencies will revalue back to the mean. The world economy functions best close to the center of gravity. It works like the swing of a pendulum.

But the world is no longer under a gold standard for benchmarking. It is replaced by the government monetary policy. Does this principle still apply? Movement of currency today still produces inflationary and deflationary effects, it can exhibit extreme swings before reverting to the mean.

Today our currency is divided into two categories, a fixed currency and a floating currency. In both environments, the exchange rate is the ratio between one currency and another. For fixed currency, central banks buy and sell local currency to maintain a fixed ratio of local currency to the U.S dollar. For floating currency, the exchange rate is still maintained, but just not at a fixed rate. Either ways induce volatilities. Under man-made monetary exchange rate, the center of gravity has no benchmarks and hence unpredictable. George Soros' principle of *reflexivity* describes that a fall in a currency tends to create a further shrinkage of demand, leading to an even sharper fall in the currency. The opposite is also true when a rise in a currency tends to create an expansion of demand inducing a higher rise.

Flow of Funds

One of the most powerful X-Ray to predict a financial crisis is called *The Flow of Funds*. It breaks down all the debts in the credit market. What does that mean? If you recall debts and credits are both sides to the same coin, one country's debt is another country's credit. So these terms can be switched back and forth to suit the context. To keep it simple, Flow of Funds breakdown a country's debt in three major categories:

1. Domestic non-financial sectors
2. Financial sectors
3. Rest of the World

The reason why Flow of Funds is so important is because if you understand which sectors is showing extraordinary growth of debts, you might foresee which sector is probably going to trigger a financial crisis.

But first, let's have a look at our debt story in U.S. since it has the largest economy in the world. I guarantee you not many people would even pay attention to this.

Money, Credit, and GDP

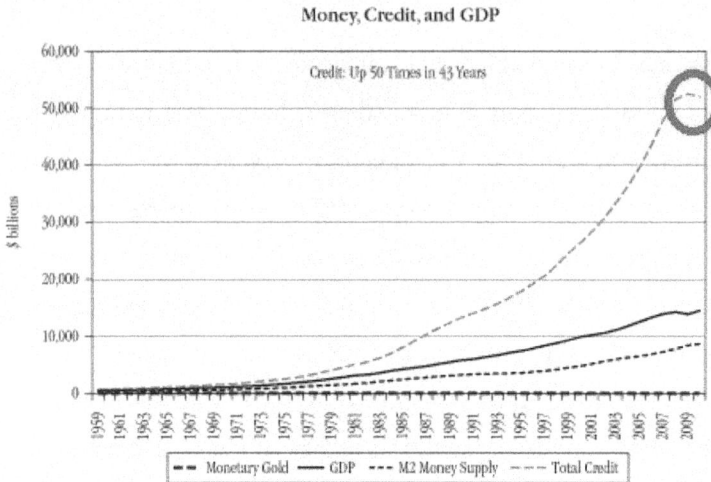

Source: Federal Reserve

The chart above is called *Total Credit Market Debt* (TCMD). It is the total amount of credits (debts) in the U.S. economy. M2 money supply is only a fraction of TCMD. But how is this chart relevant to all of us? Remember the global economy grows by exporting goods in return of the IOUs from the U.S. TCMD measures how much debts the U.S. economy accumulated to fuel the global economic growth. From the chart, you will see that TCMD in U.S. increases exponentially over the past 40 years. By 2012, TCMD hit a recorded high of $55 trillions. This explosion of credit was what changed the world.

L.1 Credit Market Debt Outstanding (1)

Billions of dollars; amounts outstanding end of period, not seasonally adjusted

		2011			2012	
		Q1	Q2	Q3	Q4	Q1	Q2
1	Total credit market debt owed by:	53804.4	53779.6	54130.1	54510.5	54868.6	55031.3
2	Domestic nonfinancial sectors	37065.4	37179.2	37662.3	38163.3	38580.6	38924.3
3	Household sector	13020.9	12935.6	12912.6	12933.7	12857.5	12895.5
4	Nonfinancial corporate business	7603.3	7753.8	7887.0	8018.1	8114.6	8228.2
5	Nonfinancial noncorporate business	3749.5	3738.2	3733.0	3751.0	3757.7	3762.0
6	State and local governments	3045.7	3013.0	3002.2	3006.8	2998.9	2988.6
7	Federal government	9645.9	9738.6	10127.6	10453.6	10851.9	11050.1
8	Rest of the world	2304.8	2326.8	2290.1	2276.7	2288.3	2268.7
9	Financial sectors	14434.2	14273.6	14177.7	14070.6	13999.7	13838.2

Source: Federal Reserve (Flow of Funds section L1)

Prior to the breakdown of the Bretton Woods, TCMD was relatively non-existent. After President Nixon closed the gold window in 1971, the nature of our economy had changed. If you examine the chart again, you will discover that the TCMD started off nice and slowly at the beginning of 1971, then it increased exponentially every year. By now, TCMD increases by more than 50 times in less than 50 years! This is where our prosperity came from. I am not opposing to the use of debt. Like the famous financial book *Rich Dad Poor Dad* said, good debt makes you rich and bad debt makes you poor. So if, you take advantages of debt, you can make a fortune.

But hang on a second. What had happened to the circle in 2008? It had shown a level off. There was a sharp contraction. This is signaling to us that there is an emergency going on right now.

Mechanism of Financial Crisis

According to *Ludwig von Mises*, there is no means of avoiding the final collapse of a boom caused by credit expansion. The inevitable mechanism is to either face a final catastrophic collapse of the currency system or face less pain by voluntary abandonment of current credit expansion. The financial crisis in the 20th century had demonstrated this principle well.

	Great Depression 1930	Japan Great Bubble 1980	Asian Financial Crisis 1997
Monetary System	Abandon Classical Gold Standard in 1914	Breakdown of Bretton Woods System	Breakdown of Bretton Woods System
Prosperity Prior to Crisis	Roaring 20s	Large Trade Surplus with U.S. and Japan	Huge Foreign Capital Inflow
Credit Expansion	Yes	Yes	Yes
Stock Market Boom	DJIA rose from 60 to 400 between 1921 to 1972	Nikkei Exchange increases 7.6 times from 1972 high	Hong Kong (^HIS) increases 64 times from 1969 low
Effect of Crisis	Bankrupts, foreclosure, Wall Street almost collapsed	Japan Enters deflationary spiral still exist today	Currency Crisis in Asian countries

Source: Author, Table showing boom and burst prior to financial crisis

The Boom is the Problem, The Burst is the Solution

Today, our money is being corrupted by government interference and Federal Reserve credit creation. Every time there is a financial crisis, instead of allowing the market to self-correct, politicians try to pop up the economy for political reasons. They become political popular by bailout companies which should have failed. They buy back toxic assets, and print currency. The expense is that future generation, or us, are paying the price through inflation, taxation and lower standard of living.

Evolution to the 21ˢᵗ Century Financial Crisis

At the beginning of the 21st century, the government had been a major player in rescuing the economy. Every time we faced a crisis, the Federal Reserve steps in.

To understand what is happening, let's look at U.S. M2 money supply below.

US M2 Money Supply (1960-2012)

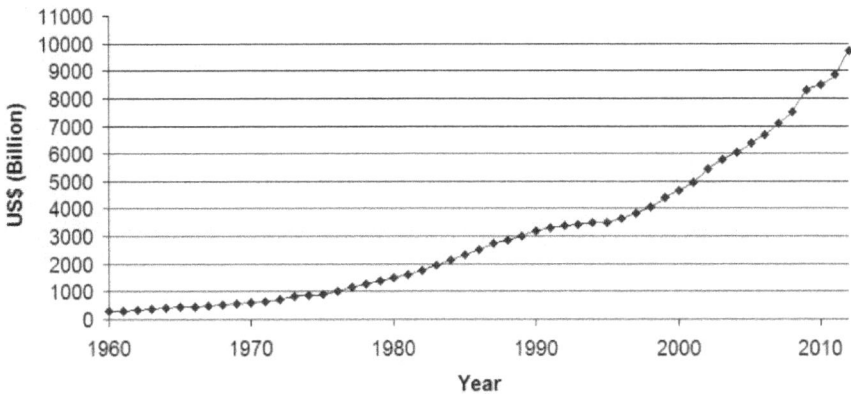

Source: Federal Reserve

Years	Increase in M2 Money Supply US %(Billion)
1961-1970	$317 Billion - $592 Billion
1971-1980	$635 Billion - $1,486 Billion
1981-1990	$1,610 Billion - $3,174 Billion
1991-2000	$3,292 Billion - $6,665 Billion
2001-2010	$4.968 Billion - $9,721 Billion

Source: Author

[**Note**: Almost every decade, the M2 money supply doubles]

M2 is the base money in our economy. It includes all the coins, banknotes, demand and time deposits. It is the amount of money in circulation. Base money is the money supply where the government can print. TCMD is the layer of the money supply where the government can just influence. They have no direct control of it. If TCMD collapses, our reality will be very different from today.

The reason why I focus on the U.S. is because this is the world's largest economy and the U.S. dollar is the world reserve currency. But I challenge if you to research the growth of M2 in your own country, you will probably end up with similar pattern- an exponential growth of money supply. So you see, for every decade, the M2 money supply doubles to keep the economy growing. So for every decade, the financial crisis will be more devastating than the previous ones.

The Dot Com

At the beginning of the 21st century, the world had a speculative bubble. Internet was relatively new to most people. There were a lot of fantasy and speculations involved in the market. Companies listed in the stock exchange market saw their stock price shoot up by simply adding a ".com" to the end of the name. Investors were built in with the perceptions that internet companies will certainly make profits, they don't even care if the company itself is going to make a profit.

NASDAQ Bubble

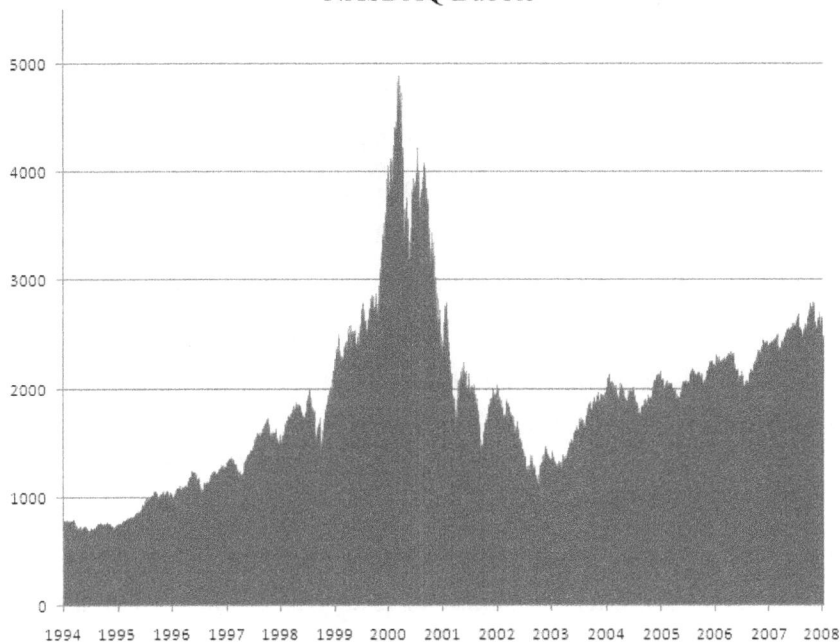

Source:Wikipedia

A lot of excitement was built in the stock market as the NASDAQ peaked at 5048. When the dot.com bubble burst. A lot of wealth vaporized. InfoSpace share price peaked $1305/share in March 2000. After the crash, it was down to $22/share. Amazon.com went from $107/share down to $7/share. Some companies' share price went to zero.

But where did all these wealth comes from? If you have a second look at the M2 money supply in the 90s, you will know the answer. The indirect catalyst of the dot.com bubble was the result of increase in M2 to perpetuate the financial crisis in the 90s. Without it, dot.com bubble will not be as devastating.

Get Blamed for Doing the Right Thing

Alan Greenspan was the Chairman of the Federal Reserve during the dot. com bubble. Decades of increase in M2 money supply causes high inflation. Things were beginning to get of control. To contain inflation, Greenspan increases the interest rate 6 times, from 4.75 percent to 6.76 percent. This was the right thing to do to slow down economic growth. However, coincidentally it burst the dot.com bubble. Public blamed Alan Greenspan for his interest rate hike. Businesses could not afford high interest payment lost money. People withdrawn from the stock market and many dot.com companies based heavily on speculations went burst.

Effects of Interest Rate

The third financial X-Ray you must pay close attention to is the interest rate. Unlike exchange rate, interest rate has a higher predictability. Right after the burst of the dot.com bubble, U.S should have a very steep recession. The magnitude of the recession should be equivalent to the boom. But the recession didn't last long at all. Government stepped in and rescued the public.

But how do they do that? They reduced the interest rate all the way to 1%. You see, interest rate is the demand and supply of money. Increase in interest rate add frictions to the economic growth as it costs businesses more to borrow. Oppositely, a cut in interest rate means businesses can borrow cheap credit and spend. Stock market will pick up in the short run as a result of that and the public can get cheap mortgages from banks.

US official interest rates

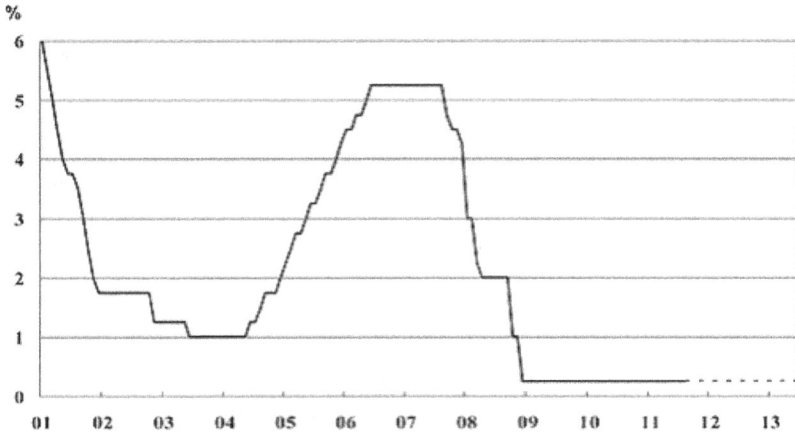

Source: http://www.stringfellow.co.za/us-updated-charts-august-2011/

The Untold Cause of Sub-prime Mortgage Crisis

When everyone thinks about the global financial crisis (GFC) of 2008, they would recall terms like mortgage backed securities (MBS), AIG, credit rating, derivatives. In Chapter 2, we had a brief looked at the aftermaths of subprime mortgage crisis. Now it is time to look at the real causes and see if we can actually predict this financial crisis using what we have learnt.

You maybe surprise that the cause of the GFC was not really because of unethical rating by credit agencies, the repackaging of MBS by banks, nor the GSE like Fannie and Freddie. They were sparks of the crisis. You see, every crisis has *sparks* and *fuels*. Without large volume of *fuels*, a *spark* can only cause a small explosion.

Years of low interest rate (2002 – 2004) helped fuelled the housing bubble in 2008. If you remembered *U.S. President George W. Bush's* speech, at the same period, he announced the increase of commitment particularly in the real estate industry. The purpose was to help everyone in American to own a home.

Here is what was said

"I believe in the American Dream. I believe there is such a thing called the America Dream and I believe those of us who were given the responsibilities must do everything we can to spotlight the dream and make sure the dream shines.....
And obviously the Federal Government has to play an important role...
And we also need to bring others into the process, particular the real estate industry..... Fannie Mae, Freddie Mac and the Federal Home Loan Bank will increase their commitment to minority market by more than $440 billion dollars."
-U.S President George W. Bush

In the *Flow of Funds*, Housing is the pillar of an economy. In 2010, it accounts for 73% ($9.95 trillion) of the debt in the non-financial sector. The home mortgage to GDP ratio was equivalent to 68.8%. So that means home mortgage alone accounts for 68.8% of all the goods and services produced in the entire year. No wonder why the U.S. government will do whatever they can to pop up the housing market.

L.100 Households and Nonprofit Organizations (1)
Billions of dollars; amounts outstanding end of period, not seasonally adjusted

		2010	2011				2012		
			Q1	Q2	Q3	Q4	Q1	Q2	
1	Total financial assets	49518.7	51339.5	51412.3	48659.7	50275.4	52668.1	51925.6	1
24	Total liabilities	13714.5	13641.0	13556.7	13474.9	13484.7	13441.2	13458.5	24
25	Credit market instruments	13137.5	13020.9	12935.6	12912.6	12933.7	12857.5	12895.5	25
26	Home mortgages (4)	9950.9	9884.7	9826.5	9773.7	9721.6	9640.0	9589.1	26
27	Consumer credit	2545.3	2512.3	2534.2	2578.6	2631.7	2619.0	2661.1	27
28	Municipal securities	262.3	261.9	260.7	256.1	254.4	252.3	247.6	28
29	Depository institution loans n.e.c. (5)	61.0	45.3	-1.0	-9.8	12.4	34.8	88.5	29
30	Other loans and advances	136.1	136.4	136.9	137.8	138.1	137.8	137.6	30
31	Commercial mortgages	181.9	180.3	178.3	176.2	175.5	173.7	171.6	31
32	Security credit	278.2	315.7	312.8	251.9	238.5	267.7	244.5	32
33	Trade payables	274.1	279.1	282.6	286.0	288.2	289.8	290.5	33
34	Deferred and unpaid life insurance premiums	24.7	25.2	25.6	24.4	24.3	26.2	28.0	34

Source: Federal Reserve

What Ways Do You See it Coming?

As i am writing now, there is an extreme disequilibrium in the global economy. Governments worldwide had been very successful at perpetuating the GFC in 2008. As U.S. continues to fuel the growth of the world economy as the powerhouse through debts, and the world continue to accept IOUs, this dilemma may continue for a little longer. We should be all feeling the effects of this dilemma right now as U.S continues to export inflation to its trading partners like China, and the Chinese continues to buy up assets like real estates all around the world and pushes the prices through the roof. I am uncertain how much longer this can be sustained. But I am sure there will be a painful correction coming.

In fact, the level off of TCMD in 2008 marked the first sight of a falling star of economic growth. Right now, the world has two ways to go. Either ways will not be a pretty picture for most people holding fiat currency and paper assets. If we are to continue the prosperity in the next 10 years like we enjoy today, the TCMD needs to double to $100 Trillion. This means the world would suffer a much, much higher inflation than what we are seeing today. This is what the government stimulus programs are doing right now. On the other hand, if the free market is allowed to seek a fair market value, and the TCMD corrects, it will be another episode of prolonged *1930 Great Depression*. Which ways do you see it coming?

Chapter 9
Who is pulling the Strings?

"Let me issue and control a nation's money supply and I care not who writes the Law."

-Mayer Amschel Rothschild

The Corruption of Real Money

Congratulate yourself if you have gone this far. At the beginning of this book, I started off with a conspiracy theory that everything happening in the society, the way we brought up and educated, the grow and crash of the economy, were all scripted. They were well designed by a social class long time ago. When these cartels pull the strings of our economy, wealth transfer happens. These cartels are called *illuminati.* They control world affairs through governments and giant corporations. The corruption of real money is their script of wealth transfer. The script is written to transfer wealth from 99% of the population indirectly to the top legally and willingly. They capitalize on the ignorance of people on money and complexity of the financial market. Socialism was their goal to enslave everyone. Fiat currency is the tool they use to accomplish their goal.

Are you feeling that already? Every financial crisis requires more currencies to bailout. Each bailout is done through taxation or inflation. Financial crisis is just a setup to transfer our wealth away from us. By no means these are accidents, it is the essence of the plan.

The New World Order -Annuit Coeptis

I want you to look this symbol for a moment. It is an upper pyramid with and an eye disconnected from the lower one. This symbol is used to portray events that are planned to take place in the real world.

The pyramid in the symbol is divided into two parts. The hidden meaning is to represent a two class society. The upper part is the ***illuminati***, which is where wealth is transferred to from the lower pyramid, which is the middleclass. Their eye, which is called the all-seeing eye of God or Eye of Providence, is always watching over the lower pyramid. *Annuit Coeptis* means favors undertakings. This one eye symbolism was placed on the dollar bill. Might this mean the U.S. dollar is deliberately designed to collapse so that the ***illuminati*** can run their scripts to transfer our wealth from all of us in the name of socialism and peace?

Illuminati Loves Chaos in the Name of Peace

In times of uncertainty, people will choose to surrender their freedom over to security. War and financial crisis are definitely times of uncertainties. These are the periods where governments gain power over people.

Wars indebted countries. Financial crisis requires bailout. Both transfers wealth away from the public. The main reason why the *Illuminati* loves chaos is because of the peace. Have i lost you already? Without chaos, the *Illuminati* cannot indebt countries. Without war, they cannot have public cry for peace. More peace means more government spending on peace keeping. More peace means government could bailout too big to fail companies to avoid chaos. In order to save the world, we must save the banks. Does any of these sound familiar to you?

The New World Order uses two mechanisms to rule the world. One is the military command in the name of peace. The other one is monetary control through the issue of one world currency nations must accept.

One World Currency

The coming financial crisis will complete the final stage of *Illuminati* grand plan. That is to have one world currency. In fact, since WWII IMF already had a supplement of foreign reserve asset called *Special Drawing Right* (SDR). SDR is not a currency itself but a claim check to currency held by IMF members. The SDR comes to prominence when the U.S. dollar is weak.

Today, U.S. dollar is in deep trouble. The subject of world currency was put on the table as an option to build the new monetary system. The *Illuminati* will convince the public that by having one world currency, there will be no more financial crisis. The truth is that having one world currency will mean a big leap towards a world government central management, Monopolies of cooperation and complete socialism.

Life Under World Government

Under world government and one world currency, there will be no high tax. It is not necessary. Everyone is working for the government. Private companies exist in the name of private companies, and most of them are nationalized. There will not be competitions. In the financial market, there will be no booms and bursts. There will be no more business cycles, and there will be no recessions or depressions.

But what's wrong with that?

Under such arrangements, this would mean the world economy will only rely on the expansion of our currency supply to grow. No competitions mean there will be no incentives to innovate. Most likely everyone would enjoy being in the service sectors. These jobs will not grow the economy. Our inflation rate will grow exponentially high. Even with a steady paycheck from the government. Our purchasing power diminishes years after years. Millions will die every day due to starvation. This will be our new normal.

Because the World Order is there for peace, so any protestors will be locked up by the world police. No one, not even the media, will dare to critic the *Illuminati*.

Under such arrangements, there will be two types of educations. One is for the *Illuminati*, and the other is for the rest of the world. The *Illuminati* education system will be based on how to maintain the world order. The rest of the world will be taught how to work hard, save money, with no aspiration but to enjoy life. The direction of our education system will be to teach to be passive and submit to the New World Order.

Will you Fight or Surrender to the System?

You might disagree with all of these, but this is a possible future scenario, and we are in the transition period right now. Can you beat the *Corruption of Real Money*? Absolutely. You still have a choice. If you have really understood the message of the *Corruption of Real Money* up to this point, you are armed with the right knowledge. My job is done. Now you need a plan and action on it while there is still time, which is the subject of my next book. As I am writing now, I see a storm approaching. We are in the period of clam before the storm. This coming decade will become completely unlike the past decade as we move from 2013 to 2023. It is as certain as sunrise.

PART II

SETTING YOUR FINANCIAL SAIL

Chapter 10

Philosopher's Legacy

"If you don't have a plan in life, chances are you'll fall into someone else's plan"
-Grandad

At a very young age, I love accompanying grandad to his usual battlefield. Don't get me wrong as I am not talking about battlefields with blood and violence. Grandad is not only a financial tactician in real life. He is also an expert in Chinese chess game. Chess game is all about plans. No plans or not good enough plans are receipts for losing.

"Ching, life is like a game of chess. To win, you must have a plan. You must refine it to fit the whole picture. You must always see the whole picture, but be prepared for the picture to change."

How to Plan?

Before building a house, the first thing you do is to call in an architect to draw up a plan. Could you imagine what will happen if you start building a house without a plan? I am fascinated to find most people plan their vacations better than their life. Maybe escape is always better than change. What do you think?

Grandad had taught me the importance of financial and life planning at a very young age. It was daunting at the beginning. Most of the time I did not know where I want to go. But after a while, through trial and error. I got experience about planning. It starts off with a dream. Life without dreams is meaningless. Do you agree? A plan is a medium to bridge you between the present and your dream. It is a vehicle to get you from where you are now and where you want to be.

How Fast is Your Plan?

Different plans have different speed. Flying in a Boeing 747 is never the same as taking a bus and stuck in traffic. Which vehicles you are taking to reach your dream is up to you. Every plan has a price. It is not measured in dollar but in terms of time. A flight in a Boeing 747 may be expensive, but it can carry you to your destination in a short period of time. Buses might be far cheaper, but it might drive you in circles or take you ages before you can arrive at your destination.

So what qualifies a good plan would mean it can take you from present to your dream within a certain time frame.

Hard Working People May Actually Be Lazy

May hard working people be lazy? Certainly yes. Most hard working people only have one plan. That is to work hard, save money, go back to school only for the purpose of a pay rise, buy a house, invest in a retirement plan. Eventually, by retirement age, they live below their means and live off a tight budget or government support.

Grandad comments them as too lazy to plan. These people are usually very hard working and smart, unfortunately, their life will go nowhere. They are victims of the corruption of real money. To them, climbing the corporate ladder is an important thing. The subject of money is to be avoided. Minding other people business is more important than their planning their life. They believe pay rise is the solution to financial problem. Promotion motivates them to move into that direction. Do you want to be one of them?

You Don't Know What You Don't Know

I remembered I was in a lecture in university, and we were learning digital electronic design. A huge leap in background knowledge prerequisite combined with the nightmarish ascent of the lecturer kept everyone in mystery about what was happening.

"Are there any questions?" The lecturer asked.

The class went dead silent.

"Very good. That means we can move on to the next chapter."

First Step: Where are You Now?

To develop a plan, it is important to know where are you today. While readers like you maybe a student still doing high school, an employee of a company, or a business owner. You may all have different background and different financial starting point. But it doesn't matter. This method is simple and it works for all age. The first step you must do is to position yourself. This can be done through the income statement on the next page. An income statement has two boxes. The upper box records all your income. The lower box records all your expenses. Below you have net saving, which basically tells you how much you have saved.

Income Statement

Income

Job
Part Time Business

Expense

Taxes
Transport
Food Expenses
Credit Card Repayment

Net Saving = Income - Expense

The habit of doing routinely is very important. The income statement is like an X-ray to diagnose your financial health. Most people only focus on income. Higher income is meaningless if a person's spending habit is reckless. At the end, only the net-saving counts.

Second Step: Don't Save Money, Save Real Money

The second step of the plan is don't save money (currency). The amount of currencies measured in dollar terms is rising because the government is printing currency and cause ragging inflation. Everything goes up except currency. Higher account balance is meaningless if it buys you less things.

The wise plan would be to save in assets. Assets which produce income for you or store values.

Balance Sheet

Assets	Liability
Gold and Silver Coins Business Book	Credit Card Loans School Loans

Gold and Silver are real money. They hedge the value of your purchasing power. It is one of the easiest type of asset to get into, especially silver. Currency is a tool to transfer your purchasing power away from you. So you do not want to hold too many of them. There are many types of assets class you can acquire. Some like real estate requires huge capital to get into while others like business requires time and experience. It is not easy but once you are heading towards this direction. You are on the right track. So the second step is to develop a plan to acquire assets.

The liability column is loans, which are basically debts incurred. Since using debts to produce income is not the subject of this book, I will not go into it.

[**Note**: This concept is inspired by *Robert Kiyosaki* on his book *Rich Dad Poor Dad.*]

Third Step: Set a Goal

Without a sense of urgency, desire loses its value. The third step is to set goals and accomplish them. You may want to set a small goal like accumulating an asset that produces as little as $10 every month. After success, celebrate. You should congratulate yourself because every small accomplishment is a step towards the final goal.

The Philosopher's Legacy

Now, you should have a basic idea to develop your own plan to defy the corruption of real money. But it is insufficient. Planning and knowledge are key elements to your goal, the main obstacle you will face is discipline. Wrong attitude or philosophy will move you to the wrong directions. The weakness of mindset is what causes failure. If you can overcome it, you are way ahead of others. This is what grandad called the philosophy legacy.

1. Defying Inaction
2. Focus
3. No Excuses
4. Turning Failure into Success

Legacy One: Defying Inaction.

Newton's first law states that an object at rest stays at rest and an object in motion stays in motion. Inaction breeds inaction. Every time I heard people say " I will do it someday." The chances are they will say the same thing again tomorrow. Beating inaction requires motivation. Once you are motivated, believe me, you can move mountains.

Legacy Two: Focus

You must focus on your plan in accumulating asset. The word focus actually has a meaning behind it, which is *Follow One Course Until Success*. In life there are a lot of things which keep you away from your focus. The more focus (time) you put in building your asset column, the faster you will see your results.

Legacy Three: No Excuses

One of the most powerful obstacles in your plan is the phase "Yes, But...". It is powerful because it is typically how people think. It is as if they are purposely trying to find a way which does not work. Please try to break this habit. There are no risk free decisions in life. Everything has an opportunity cost.

Legacy Four: Turning Failure into Success

Most likely, some of your plans works and some do not in the first go. You will have low moments. I tasted the bitter feeling of failure. I know how it feels. Some people might choose to give up on their plan. Don't be one of them. Failure is not permanent. No one failed permanently. It defies the law of averages. If you plan and action on it frequently enough, a ratio will appear. Sometimes you succeed and sometimes you don't. If you learn from your mistake, the chances are that this ratio improves. You will have the Midas touch of success.

Take Actions!

The concept of philosophy legacy is simple but it is difficult to put into action, it is all up to you how you want to defy the corruption of real money. Are you willing to hold currency and watch your wealth continues to lose value? Or you choose to invest time to accumulate assets? Every dollar you spend every decision you made writes your financial destiny.

Chapter 11
Setting your Sail

Finally, I would like to thank all of you for reading this book. It is a long journey. I hope I demystify the subject of money in an unconventional and fun way. More importantly, I hope you all enjoy reading it.

Before closing this book, I wish to share with you my final thoughts on life planning. I know all of you come from a very different background, different age, and perhaps different cultures. Everyone is shaped with different experiences. Maybe you are born fortunate, maybe you are not. If you have a unfair beginning, don't let your present decides your future. Do fight back. You are the author of your future. It is not what happened which determines your future. It is what you do about what happened. Think of your life as a sail boat, it is not the blowing of the wind that determines your destination. It is the set of the sail. The same wind blows on us all, whether it is the wind of disasters, the wind of opportunity, the wind of change, the wind when it is favorable and unfavorable. The secret is that the destination of your arrival is not the blowing of the wind, but the set of your sail. I wish you all for the best sail in this coming decade. I will see you at your destination.

Recommended Readings
To further enhance your financial diligent

Economy

Man Economy and State with Power and Market **(Murray N. Rothbard)**

America's Great Depression **(Murray N. Rothbard)**

Crash Proof **(Peter D. Schiff)**

Free to Choose **(Milton Friedman and Rose Friedman)**

The Dollar Crisis **(Richard Duncan)**

Corruption of Capitalism **(Richard Duncan)**

Human Action **(Ludwig Von Mises)**

Monetary History and Money

Gold **(Nathan Lewis)**

A Primer on Money, Banking and Gold **(Peter L. Bernstein)**

Guide to Investing in Gold and Silver **(Michael Maloney)**

A Monetary History of the United States, 1857-1960 **(Milton Friedman)**

The Federal Reserve

End the Fed **(Ron Paul)**

The Creature of Jekyll Island **(G. Edward Griffin)**

The Case against the Fed **(Murray N. Rothbard)**

About the Author

Marco Chu Kwan Ching
Author, Investor

I began my profession as an electrical engineer in TOSHIBA after graduated from *The University of New South Wales* (UNSW) in 2009. I had a small web design business which was for indexing restaurants. I was firmly sitting on the dream of most undergraduates- a job and a part time business. With the collapse of the global economy since 2008, I first noticed how the effects of the financial crisis unfold . I experienced the accelerating inflation rapidly eroding our wealth, I witnessed the foreclosures of businesses, income polarization,   the interventions of the government monetary policies. Even with little life experience on these subjects, I know something is not right. The current financial system is developing cracks. This sparked my interest in studying monetary history and the global economy. I set out to research the answers myself.

What I found shocked me to my core. The root of all the problems lies within our philosophy of money. The definition of money is flawed. Currency is not money. The original idea of money being a container to store the value of our labour, time, ideas, talents, are replaced by debts. Money, rather than being a store of value, becomes a plan to transfer our wealth away from us. My mission is to educate as many people as possible about these findings, so they are armed with the right knowledge to protect themselves and their family from this corrupted monetary system. That's why I am willing to give up my time to work on the material that now appears in *The Corruption of Real Money*.

www.ingramcontent.com/pod-product-compliance
Lightning Source LLC
Chambersburg PA
CBHW031956190326
41520CB00007B/264